PRIVATE SCHOOLS

of the

SAN FRANCISCO PENINSULA &

SILICON VALLEY

(Elementary & Middle)

BY

ELLEN S. LUSSIER

pince-nez press

Private Schools of the San Francisco Peninsula & Silicon Valley (Elementary & Middle)

ISBN 0-9648757-6-4
Library of Congress Catalog Card No.: 00-106851
Printed in the United States.

pince-nez press
1459 18th Street, PMB 175
San Francisco, California 94107
415.267.5978
www.pince-nez.com
info@pince-nez.com

ACKNOWLEDGMENTS

Although this book lists one author, it truly is the product of a team effort and could not have been completed without the guidance and persistence of my editor, Susan Vogel. I also wish to thank all of the admission directors who carved out some of their limited time to complete the questionnaires and to show me their schools—without their input there simply would be no book. I must also thank Christine Metropoulos, who took over the tedious task of re-typing the school profiles in a consistent format when my word processing skills reached their limit. Finally, I'd like to thank my family: My husband, Jim, for never questioning why I chose writing this book over the practice of law, and my children, Michael and Danielle, whose interest and pride in my book project has meant the most to me.

DEDICATION

To Michael and Danielle

TABLE OF CONTENTS

School Lists

Introduction

Schools

166	Our Lady of Perpetual Help School*
166	Peninsula School*
101	The Phillips Brooks School
103	Pinewood
171	Primary Plus*
105	Queen of Apostles School
107	Redeemer Lutheran School
172	Resurrection School*
172	Sacred Heart School*
172	St. Andrew's Episcopal School*
110	St. Catherine of Siena School
113	St. Charles School
173	St. Christopher School*
173	St. Clare's School*
174	St. Cyperian Elementary School*
167	St. Dunston School*
174	St. Elizabeth Seton School*
174	St. Francis Cabrini School*
117	St. Gregory School
175	St. John the Baptist School*
175	St. John Vianney School*
119	St. Joseph of Cupertino School
176	St. Joseph Elementary (Mountain View)*
123	St. Joseph's School (Atherton)
126	St. Justin School
129	St. Lawrence Elementary & Middle School
176	St. Leo the Great Elementary School*
132	St. Lucy School
134	St. Martin School
137	St. Martin of Tours Elementary School
176	St. Mary's School*
167	St. Matthew's Catholic School*
140	St. Matthew's Episcopal Day School
177	St. Nicholas School*
177	St. Patrick School*
167	St. Pius School*
167	St. Raymond School*
168	St. Robert School*
178	St. Simon School*
168	St. Veronica School*
144	St. Victor School
178	Sierra School*
178	Silicon Valley Academy*
178	Southbay Christian School*
147	South Peninsula Hebrew Day School*

168	Stanbridge Academy*
148	Trinity School
179	Valley Christian Schools*
151	Waldorf School of the Peninsula
155	Woodland School
158	Woodside Priory School
179	Yavneh Day School*

* = short listings

Schools By City/Town

Atherton

Menlo School
St. Joseph's School

Belmont

Charles Armstrong School*
Immaculate Heart of Mary School*
Notre Dame Elementary School

Burlingame

Our Lady of Angels*
St. Catherine of Siena School

Campbell

St. Lucy School

Colma

Holy Angels School*

Cupertino

St. Joseph's of Cupertino School

Daly City

The Hilldale School
Our Lady of Mercy School*
Our Lady of Perpetual Help School*

Foster City

Jewish Day School of the North Peninsula

HILLSBOROUGH

Crystal Springs Uplands School
Nueva School

LOS ALTOS

Canterbury Christian*
Los Altos Christian School
Pinewood School
St. Nicholas School*
St. Simon School*
Waldorf School of the Peninsula

LOS GATOS

Hillbrook School*
St. Mary's School*
Yavneh Day School*

MENLO PARK

German-American School of San Francisco*
Nativity Elementary*
Peninsula School*
The Phillips Brooks School
St. Raymond School*
Trinity School

MILLBRAE

St. Dunston School*

MILPITAS

St. John the Baptist School*

MOUNTAIN VIEW

Canyon Heights Academy*
German School of Silicon Valley*
The Girls' Middle School
St. Joseph Elementary*
Southbay Christian School*

PACIFICA

Alma Heights Christian Academy*
Good Shepherd School*

Palo Alto

Castilleja School
Challenger School*
Children's International School
Emerson School*
International School of the Peninsula*
Keys School
Mid-Peninsula Jewish Community Day School
St. Elizabeth Seton School*

Portola Valley

Woodland School
Woodside Priory School

Redwood City

Heritage Christian Academy*
Our Lady of Mount Carmel School*
Redeemer Lutheran School
St. Pius Elementary*

San Bruno

Highland Christian School*
St. Robert School*

San Carlos

Alpha Beacon Christian School*
St. Charles School

San Jose

Challenger School*
Christian Community Academy*
Five Wounds School
The Harker School
Holy Family Education Center
Holy Spirit Elementary School*
Milpitas Christian School*
Most Holy Trinity School
Primary Plus School*
Queen of Apostles School
St. Christopher School*
St. Francis Cabrini School
St. John Vianney School

St. Leo the Great Elementary School*
St. Martin of Tours Elementary School
St. Patrick School
St. Victor School
Valley Christian School*

SAN MATEO

The Carey School
Odyssey School
St. Gregory School
St. Matthew's Catholic School*
St. Matthew's Episcopal Day School
Stanbridge Academy*

SANTA CLARA

St. Clare's School*
St. Justin School
St. Lawrence Elementary & Middle School
Sierra School*

SARATOGA

Sacred Heart School*
St. Andrew's Episcopal School*

SOUTH SAN FRANCISCO

All Souls Catholic Elementary School*
Mater Dolorosa Elementary School*
St. Veronica School*

SUNNYVALE

Challenger School*
French American School of Silicon Valley*
Resurrection School*
St. Cyperian Elementary School*
St. Martin School
Silicon Valley Academy*
South Peninsula Hebrew Day School

* = short listings

SCHOOLS BY TYPE– RELIGIOUS OR NONSECTARIAN

NON-SECTARIAN

The Carey School
Castilleja School
Challenger School*
Charles Armstrong School*
Children's International School
Crystal Springs Uplands School
Emerson School*
French American School of Silicon Valley*
German-American School of San Francisco*
The Girls' Middle School
The Harker School
Hillbrook School
The Hilldale School
International School of the Peninsula*
Keys School
Menlo School
Nueva School
Odyssey School
Peninsula School*
The Phillips Brooks School
Pinewood
Primary Plus*
Sierra School*
Stanbridge Academy
Waldorf School of the Peninsula
Woodland School

INDEPENDENT RELIGIOUS SCHOOLS

Canyon Heights Academy*
Notre Dame Elementary School
St. Andrew's Episcopal School
St. Joseph's School (Atherton)
St. Matthew's Episcopal Day School
Trinity School
Woodside Priory School

CATHOLIC PAROCHIAL SCHOOLS

Under Archdiocese of San Francisco:

All Souls Catholic Elementary School*
Holy Angels School*
Immaculate Heart of Mary School*
Mater Dolorosa School*
Nativity Elementary*
Our Lady of Angels School*
Our Lady of Mercy School*
Our Lady of Mount Carmel School*
Our Lady of Perpetual Help School*
St. Catherine of Siena School
St. Charles School
St. Dunston School*
St. Gregory School
St. Matthew's Catholic School*
St. Pius School*
St. Raymond School
St. Robert School*
St. Veronica School*

Under Diocese of San Jose:

Five Wounds School
Holy Family Education Center
Holy Spirit Elementary School*
Most Holy Trinity School
Queen of Apostles School
Resurrection School*
Sacred Heart School*
St. Christopher School*
St. Clare's School*
St. Cyperian Elementary School*
St. Elizabeth Seton School*
St. Francis Cabrini School*
St. John the Baptist School*
St. John Vianney School*
St. Joseph of Cupertino School
St. Joseph Elementary School*
St. Justin School
St. Lawrence Elementary & Middle School
St. Leo the Great Elementary School*
St. Lucy School
St. Martin School

St. Martin of Tours Elementary School
St. Mary's School*
St. Nicholas School*
St. Patrick School*
St. Simon School*
St. Victor School

OTHER CHRISTIAN SCHOOLS

Alpha Beacon Christian School*
Alma Heights Christian School*
Canterbury Christian*
Christian Community Academy*
Good Shepherd School*
Heritage Christian Academy*
Highlands Christian School*
Los Altos Christian School
Milpitas Christian School*
Redeemer Lutheran School
Southbay Christian School*
Valley Christian School*

JEWISH SCHOOLS

Jewish Day School of the North Peninsula*
Mid-Peninsula Jewish Community Day School
South Peninsula Hebrew Day School*
Yavneh Day School*

* = short listings

SCHOOLS BY ACCREDITATION

ACCREDITED BY CAIS (SOURCE: CAIS)

The Carey School
Castilleja School
Crystal Springs Uplands School
The Harker School
Hillbrook School*
International School of the Peninsula*
Jewish Day School of the North Peninsula^
Keys School
Menlo School
Mid-Peninsula Jewish Community Day School^

Nueva School
The Phillips Brooks School
St. Andrew's Episcopal School
St. Joseph's School
St. Matthew's Episcopal Day School
South Peninsula Hebrew Day School^*
Trinity School
Woodside Priory School
Yavneh Day School^*
^= Provisional member

ACCREDITED BY **WASC** (SOURCE: **WASC**)

Charles Armstrong School^*
The Girls' Middle School^
Good Shepherd School*
Los Altos Christian School
Milpitas Christian School*
Notre Dame Elementary School
Pinewood (G7-12)
Redeemer Lutheran School
Sierra School^*
South Bay Christian School*
Stanbridge Academy*
Valley Christian Schools*
^ = Candidates for accreditation

ACCREDITED BY **WASC/WCEA**

All Souls Catholic Elementary School*
Five Wounds School
Holy Angels School*
Holy Family Education Center
Holy Spirit Elementary School*
Immaculate Heart of Mary School*
Mater Dolorosa School*
Most Holy Trinity School
Nativity Elementary School*
Notre Dame Elementary School
Our Lady of Angels School*
Our Lady of Mercy School*
Our Lady of Mount Carmel School*
Our Lady of Perpetual Help School*
Queen of Apostles School
Resurrection School*
Sacred Heart School*

St. Catherine of Siena School
St. Charles School
St. Christopher School*
St. Clare's School*
St. Cyperian School*
St. Dunston School*
St. Elizabeth Seton School*
St. Francis Cabrini School*
St. Gregory School
St. John the Baptist School*
St. John Vianney School*
St. Joseph of Cupertino School
St. Joseph Elementary School*
St. Justin School
St. Lawrence Elementary & Middle School
St. Leo the Great Elementary School*
St. Lucy School
St. Martin School
St. Martin of Tours Elementary School
St. Mary's School*
St. Matthew School*
St. Matthew Catholic School*
St. Nicholas School*
St. Patrick School*
St. Pius School*
St. Raymond School*
St. Robert School*
St. Simon School*
St. Veronica School*
St. Victor School

Accredited by ACSI

Alma Heights Christian School*
Alpha Beacon Christian School*
Christian Community Academy*
Heritage Christian Academy*
Highlands Christian School*

* = short listings

OTHER DISTINGUISHING ASPECTS

BOARDING

The Harker School (G5-8)
Woodside Priory (co-ed G6-12 school, boarding for boys in G9-12)

ALL GIRLS

Castilleja School
The Girls' Middle School
Notre Dame Elementary

ALL BOYS

No K-8 boys' schools in the Peninsula/Silicon Valley area. See Town School for
Boys, Cathedral School for Boys, and Stuart Hall in San Francisco.

ELEMENTARY SCHOOLS WITH PRESCHOOLS

The Carey School
Five Wounds School (affiliated)
Holy Family Education Center
Los Altos Christian School
Notre Dame Elementary (same campus)
Nueva School
The Phillips Brooks School
St. Gregory School
St. Joseph's School (Atherton)
St. Lawrence Elementary
St. Martin School
St. Matthew's Episcopal Day School
South Peninsula Hebrew Day School
Trinity School
Waldorf School of the Peninsula (Young Kindergarten)
Woodland School

MIDDLE SCHOOLS (w/HIGH SCHOOLS)

Castilleja School
Crystal Springs Uplands School
Menlo School
Woodside Priory

K-8 SCHOOLS WITH HIGH SCHOOLS

[Ed. Note: Admission usually not automatic; preference may be given]

The Harker School (San Jose)
Notre Dame Elementary/Notre Dame High School (Belmont, girls)
Pinewood School (Los Altos)
St. Joseph's/Sacred Heart Preparatory (Atherton)
St. Lawrence Elementary School/St. Lawrence Academy (Santa Clara)

SCHOOLS WITH SPECIAL PROGRAMS FOR STUDENTS WITH LEARNING DISABILITIES

Charles Armstrong School*
Los Altos Christian School (Learning Assistance Dept.)
Stanbridge Academy*

ABBREVIATIONS

ASCI	Associated Christian Schools International
BAIHS	Bay Area Independent High Schools
CAIS	California Association of Independent Schools
DARE	Drug Abuse Resistance Education
ERB	Educational Records Bureau (standardized test)
ETS	Educational Testing Service
f/t	full-time
GPAC	Girls Parochial Athletic Conference
G	grade
HSPT	High School Placement Test
ISEE	Independent Schools Entrance Exam
K	Kindergarten
K-8	Kindergarten through 8th grade
N/A	Not available
N/P	Not provided
NAIS	National Association of Independent Schools
PSAT	Preliminary Scholarship Assessment Test
p/t	part-time
SAT	Stanford Achievement Test/Scholastic Assessment Test
SSAT	Secondary School Admission Test
SF	San Francisco
SPCAL	South Peninsula Catholic Athletic League
SSS	School and Student Services
WASC	Western Association of Schools and Colleges
WCEA	Western Catholic Education Association

BAY AREA HIGH SCHOOLS
REFERRED TO IN THIS BOOK

INDEPENDENT (CAIS) SCHOOLS

Athenian: The Athenian School (Danville—East Bay, co-ed)
Branson: The Branson School (Ross—Marin County, co-ed)
Castilleja: Castilleja School (Palo Alto, girls)
Convent: Convent of the Sacred Heart (SF, girls)
Crystal: Crystal Springs Uplands School (Hillsborough, co-ed)
IHS: International High School of the French-American Int'l School (SF, co-ed)
Lick-Wilmerding: Lick-Wilmerding High School (SF, co-ed)
Menlo: Menlo School (Atherton, co-ed)
SF Waldorf: San Francisco Waldorf High School (SF, co-ed)
Sacred Heart: Sacred Heart Preparatory (Atherton, co-ed)
University: University High School (San Francisco, co-ed)
Woodside Priory: Woodside Priory School (Portola Valley, co-ed)

CATHOLIC SCHOOLS

Bellarmine: Bellarmine College Preparatory (San Jose, boys)
Mercy-Burlingame: Mercy High School (Burlingame, girls)
Mercy-SF: Mercy High School (SF, girls)
Mitty: Archbishop Mitty High School (San Jose, co-ed)
Notre Dame: Notre Dame High School (Belmont, girls)
Presentation: Presentation High School (San Jose, girls)
Serra: Junipero Serra High School (San Mateo, boys)
St. Francis: St. Francis High School (Mountain View, co-ed)
St. Ignatius: St. Ignatius College Preparatory (San Francisco, co-ed)
St. Lawrence: St. Lawrence Academy (Santa Clara, co-ed)

[Ed. Note: Information on these and other private (independent and parochial) Bay Area high schools can be found in *Private High Schools of the San Francisco Bay Area (Second Edition)*, published by Pince-Nez Press. See the last pages of this book for more information.]

Crystal Springs Uplands School

INTRODUCTION

Applications to private schools in the San Francisco Peninsula/Silicon Valley area have increased dramatically over recent years, with some schools receiving more than five applications for every opening. The reasons for the increase in applications are numerous, and are not likely to change in the foreseeable future. At the top of the list, the area has a growing school age population and, due to the growing prosperity of the region, more families are willing and able to pay private school tuition. In addition, although more difficult to measure, is a growing interest in what different private schools can offer, whether it be a more rigorous academic program, a religious component, single sex education, or instruction in a subject area not provided in the public schools.

Sorting out the private school options can be confusing, time consuming, and discouraging. The purpose of this book is to provide valuable and time saving information about your private elementary and middle school options in the San Francisco Peninsula/Silicon Valley area. This book, however, does not rank or rate the schools—something that is nearly impossible to do in an objective, uniform manner. For one thing, private school students do not all take the same standardized tests as do public school students (nor are many private schools required or inclined to share their test data). Furthermore, by their very nature, many of the private schools in this book are defined by a particular focus, which may make the school perfect for one child and totally inappropriate for another. Some readers may choose to rate schools according to the school's success in placing its graduates in certain middle and high schools. Others may be more concerned with criteria such as classroom size, foreign language instruction or ethnic balance. Readers must make their own evaluations based on their own priorities.

A note for those interested solely in middle schools: This book is part of a series of books about private schools published by Pince-Nez Press. One of the books, **Private High Schools of the San Francisco Bay Area** (Second Edition), by Susan Vogel (the "High School Book"), profiles more than 50 high schools throughout the Bay Area (Marin to San Jose and the East Bay) including 22 high schools with middle schools. This book covers a more limited geographic area (Santa Clara and San Mateo counties) than the High School Book, but spans grades K-8. As a result, there is some overlap with the High School Book's coverage of those schools that have a grade 6-12 program. Readers who are interested in the high school programs of those schools should consult the High School book too. (See the order form at the back of the book or the publisher's web site at www.pince-nez.com)

MAKING THE PRIVATE SCHOOL CHOICE

THE PRIVATE SCHOOL "PIECE" OF THE EDUCATIONAL PICTURE.

The label "private school" conjures up a multitude of impressions. To some, the first image that comes to mind is a traditional one—ivy covered walls, mansion-like buildings and children in uniforms. To others, a private school represents an opportunity to choose a teaching environment and methodology that is different than that offered in a public school, or a place where the curriculum is influenced, if not guided by, religious beliefs. Whatever your reasons for considering private school, in making that choice you are also making a statement that public school does not meet your needs. Many families are, at least initially, uncomfortable with that step. After all, the California public school system (particularly the suburban districts) once enjoyed a good reputation, and many of us attended these schools, graduated, attended good colleges and turned out just fine. However natural (or strange) it may feel to be considering private school, the true anxiety sets in for many parents when they are faced with the extreme disparity between available spaces and applications.

One might think that the intense demand for private schools would result in the establishment of new private schools. Over time that may occur, but at present, of the CAIS member schools profiled in this book, half were founded over 40 years ago, and none was founded after 1978. (Proposition 13, which eliminated the power of local school boards to determine their own property tax increases, and is blamed by some as a major cause of the decline of the California public schools, was passed in 1978). Of course, starting a school requires a colossal effort and massive amounts of money, not to mention a leap of faith on the part of parents who choose to enroll their children in the early, pre-accreditation phase.

How Private School Can Shape Your Family's Life.

Whether or not you feel that you have the luxury of choice between public school and private schools with comparable academic standards, you may wish to consider how the choice between the two will affect other dimensions of your child's and your family's life.

The School as a Community.

In many areas, the neighborhood school to which every child walks or rides his bicycle is merely a piece of nostalgia—it has vanished with the apricot orchards that once covered the valley. So, to a large extent, that type of local, community school experience—where your child may go to school with friends from across the street—is difficult to come by even if your child attends a public school. Nonetheless, attending a private school will likely extend even more the geographic area from which your child will build a community of friends. If your child attends a private school, many of her friends will live outside of your neighborhood, in other towns, and some even across the Bay. This can take some of the spontaneity out of after-school play dates and turn parents and caregivers into full-time chauffeurs. On the other hand, at some private schools, many children, as they get older, end up participating in the after-school program so that they can be with their friends. This can be an especially win-win situation for working parents who otherwise would be struggling to find ways to shuttle their children around town to various activities; it creates a safe community to replace the close-knit neighborhood environment that is so difficult to find.

MAKE UP OF STUDENT BODY.

The friends your child makes at private school will be from a group of children selected by the school on the basis that the child or his family meet certain criteria set by the school, such as a shared philosophy about child development, religious beliefs, or academic achievement. This feature—a self-selected population—is one of the main differences between private and public schools. This does not necessarily mean that you will be deprived of the greater diversity (racial, socio-economic, or otherwise) expected in a public school. Bay Area public school districts with the highest test scores (as well as other measures of achievement, such as California Distinguished School awards) tend to be in the neighborhoods with the highest home prices, and many of these neighborhoods are relatively homogeneous in terms of race and ethnicity. (Some of these districts participate in voluntary transfer programs that can offset the lack of diversity somewhat.) Private schools, on the other hand, may strive to maintain an ethnic balance in admission.

SIZE OF STUDENT BODY.

Often, the total number of students enrolled in a private school is lower than you will find in a public school, and if it is a K-8 program, your child will be with that small group and on the same campus for nine years (longer, if your child starts in preschool). This provides a tremendous sense of security to many children; others may feel bored or stifled by the sameness. Give this some thought. If you are selecting a school with 20 children per grade, your boy or girl will have approximately nine other children of their same gender to play with over the years. (Your preschool girl may play with boys now, but probably won't by second grade.) On the other hand, some experts believe that the introduction of new peers in the middle school years could be a factor influencing inappropriate behavior in some teens, such as drug and alcohol use, and advise deferring a transition to a larger group until later.

SOURCES OF INFORMATION & EXPLANATION OF SUBJECTS COVERED

The majority of the information in the school profiles was gathered through responses to lengthy questionnaires sent to more than 60 schools in the area, and in many cases, through visits to the school. Additional information was obtained from the schools' own published materials, web sites and from public sources and interviews with admission directors and principals. "N/P" for "not provided," indicates that the school gave no response to the question asked. Some of the questions posed in the questionnaire resulted in subjective or promotional kinds of responses. Such information is included in quotes.

It was impossible to publish a full profile of every school in the Peninsula/Silicon Valley region. The short entries at the back of this book include schools that we were not able to include in this first edition for various reasons. In the absence of information supplied by the school, publicly available information was used, including information supplied by the school to the State Department of Education. Schools with short listings may request to have a full listing in future years by calling Pince-Nez Press at (415) 267-5978, or by sending an e-mail to info@pince-nez.com.

Although some of the school administrators who spent the considerable time required to complete the full questionnaire and to provide a private tour may have their doubts, every question was asked for a reason, with the concerns of parents in mind. With the goal of providing a comprehensive profile, we asked for information concerning everything from admissions criteria and tuition to homework policies and where the school's graduates end up for middle and high school.

GENERAL

This section of questions asked for the basics, including whether the school is single-sex or co-ed, and whether it has a religious affiliation or is nonsectarian. It asked for accreditation status and enrollment. We thought it would be good to know, in the case of a school with a religious affiliation, the percentage of students of that faith enrolled in the school. Generally, the lower the percentage, the greater the likelihood that a family whose affiliation does not match the school's will still feel comfortable with the school (and have a chance of being admitted). In this section, we also asked about average class size, a topic that has received considerable attention in the public school system over the past few years with the implementation of the Classroom Reduction Act and follow-up studies that indicate that reducing class size improves academic performance at the primary grade level. (The Classroom Reduction Act is legislation requiring that public school classes for grades K-3 have no more than 20 students per teacher.) Private schools are not required to comply with this law (although many of the independent schools have always kept their class sizes on the small side or double their teaching staff to keep a low student-teacher ratio), and we found a wide range of class sizes among the responding schools.

Length of school year is also a topic of recent attention, with the growing belief of many policy makers, educators and parents that a longer school year is essential in order to remain competitive and meet their educational goals. Most schools fall within the 170 to 180 instructional day range. (California requires 180 for public schools but has no requirement for private schools.) Length of school day can also vary, particularly in the kindergarten year, which, in public schools, can be as short as three hours. It is more typical of the private schools profiled in this book to provide a longer kindergarten day and, in some cases, to carry that through to longer days throughout the grades. Many parents feel that their children, already veterans of active preschool programs, are ready for a full day of school.

ACCREDITATION

This refers to a process of reviewing schools and their programs and deeming them as having met certain criteria. Private schools are neither required to seek accreditation nor are they required to be accredited. However, accreditation can provide parents with some level of assurance that, in the eyes of a skilled observer the school is meeting its educational goals and objectives, as well as criteria established by the accrediting agency. Further, if the possibility exists that your child may be entering a public school at some point, keep in mind that public schools have the option of refusing to accept credits from schools that are not accredited.

The oldest, most widely recognized accrediting agency is the Western Association of Schools and Colleges (WASC), one of six regional accrediting agencies nationwide that is authorized by the U.S. Department of Education to accredit schools and colleges. Their accrediting process involves the school performing an extensive "self-study" and a visit of approximately three days to the school by representatives from other schools in the region. WASC gives terms of accreditation of up to 6 years. If the school has not yet met accrediting standards but is still seeking accreditation, it will be deemed a "candidate" for WASC accreditation.

The California Association of Independent Schools (CAIS) also has an accrediting process for its own member schools. (To be a full member of CAIS, the school has to have attained accreditation through their process.) To be eligible, schools must have been in existence for six years—up until that time they can be "provisional" members. (Independent schools have the option of seeking accreditation through WASC alone, WASC and CAIS together, or CAIS alone.)

WASC also works jointly with the Association of Christian Schools International (ACSI) and the Western Catholic Education Association (WCEA) to jointly accredit their member schools. (All Catholic parochial schools in the Archdiocese of San Francisco and the Diocese of San Jose seek joint accreditation by WASC/WCEA.) Some of the schools seek the accreditation of those membership organizations alone, rather than jointly with or solely with WASC.

Some school administrators choose not to go through the accreditation process because of the time and expense involved or because they prefer that others not interfere with how they run their school. These schools sometimes point to other measures of success, including high school placements of graduates, satisfaction of parents or the school's longevity, as evidence of its achievement of high educational standards. If you are considering a school that is not accredited, you should explore the reasons why the school has not sought or attained accreditation. Also, if a school says it's accredited, ask by whom.

For further information regarding WASC and CAIS accreditation, contact the Accrediting Commission for Schools (for WASC) at (650) 696-1060 (or wascweb.org) or the CAIS at (310) 393-5161 (caisca.org). ACSI's web site is at www.acsi.org.

STUDENT BODY

We asked each school to provide a percentage breakdown of the ethnicity of its student body. This information may be important to parents who are looking for a school with ethnic diversity or one that reflects their own ethnicity or culture. Interestingly, because many of our suburban towns already tend towards ethnic homogeneity, some of the private schools may provide more ethnic diversity than do the neighborhood public schools. More important than statistics, though, is finding out if the school meets your own expectations in this regard when you visit.

We also asked for geographic information. This is of practical help, so that you'll know if you can reasonably expect to arrange car pools and play dates with families nearby. Symptomatic of the great demand for high quality private schools, parents are willing to drive significant distances to take their children to a particular school. Only a few schools have boarding students, and some of the schools that offered boarding at one time now fill their classes with local day students. Finally, in this category, we asked for estimates of households with two working parents and of single parent households. We have found that if the school has a high percentage of families in which both parents work full-time, it likely will have more flexibility and willingness to schedule its parent activities, such as parent-teacher conferences and parent participation activities, outside of business hours. Further, in schools where most parents work, the after-school program may be more well-attended and popular and therefore more interesting to your child (rather than simply a room where she and a handful of others wait out the final hours until mom or dad picks them up). Schools that truly cater to working parents will require that the children complete their homework in the extended care program and will have a teacher available to answer questions.

ADMISSION

This section contains the basics for kindergarten and other grade level admission, including application deadlines, minimum age requirement (which for many private schools is a few months older than the public school minimum age), application fee, testing and application process. In this section, we have also asked the schools to describe, in their own words, what kind of student they are looking for and the type of student the school best serves. (Of course, all schools seem to want children who "love to learn.") Finally, we asked for the number of applications received and the number of spaces in the kindergarten (or entering grade level). A word of caution about these numbers: You may find it discouraging to see ratios such as 4 to 5 applications for each space, but bear in mind that most families submit applications to multiple schools, particularly when seeking admission to schools at which the admission picture is more competitive.

Most schools will give at least some degree of preference to siblings, children of faculty and/or to children of alumni ("legacies"). Some schools will tell you during the tour or application process approximately how many of those applicants are in the pool. Schools often seek a "balanced class," in terms of numbers of boys and girls, and sometimes in terms of ethnicity and even personality (shy vs. outgoing, etc.). Finally, several of the schools profiled in this book operate their own preschools which, in some cases, become "feeders" to the kindergarten and effectively preclude newcomers, and in other cases do not fill the kindergarten class either due to the draw of a particularly strong public school in the area, or to a larger kindergarten class size. For all of these reasons, your child's prospects of admission may have less to do with his or her own attributes than with the characteristics of the students who are already chosen or being given preference.

The role of socio-economic factors in the admission decision is a sensitive subject with many schools, and none would like to admit outright that applicants from wealthy families get preference. The reality is that schools rely heavily on contributions of current families and alumni to finance operating expense shortfalls, endowments and capital campaigns. It's safe to assume that the prospect of benefiting from future donations is given some degree of consideration in the admissions process, especially when a school is deciding between two equally qualified applicants. In other words, if you can contribute a building, it probably doesn't hurt to make sure the school knows. If, like most applicants, you are not in that league, emphasize what you can bring to the school through your time and skills. (Schools need high-tech parents to help with technology programs, event planners to run the annual fundraiser, environmentalists to add dimension to the annual camping trip, etc.)

The admission season begins in early fall with school tours and open houses and ends, usually in mid-March, with notification letters. Many Catholic parochial schools schedule their parent visits in January during National Catholic Schools Week, when schools are open all day for parents to tour.

It is important to begin the process early. After you have reviewed the information in this book, contact the schools you are interested in for their admission packages and to schedule a tour or attendance at an open house. Some schools have an application deadline of December but hold tours and screenings through January. At many schools, parents are expected to submit the application (and fee) prior to attending the tour, then withdraw the application if, after the tour, they are not interested in the school. Note that application fees are normally not refundable unless you withdraw your application before it is processed.

School tours are time-consuming and often inconveniently scheduled but essential because they give you a feel for the school and an opportunity to see the school in action. Some schools are a beehive of activity with students busy working cooperatively on projects, others offer a more formal setting with children working alone at individual desks. Although parents' immediate concern is usually kindergarten and lower grades, parents can learn a lot about the schools from observing the upper grades and should not hesitate to view these while on tour. After all, the graduates are the end product of the school. Make sure that you are satisfied with the behavior, language, and attitudes of these students as well as their academic performance, for all of these can be fairly accurate predictors of what the school will do for your child.

Children are often screened or evaluated as part of the admission process, though the event is usually presented to the child as a playtime. Many schools look for "readiness," meaning whether the child has achieved the level of development of most children of the same age. This may include an assessment of basic knowledge (recognition of the alphabet, ability to recognize/write name, count, etc.) and social abilities (following directions, playing cooperatively). Parents who worry about their child's performance and who interrogate the child about "what went on in there" must be careful not to telegraph their anxiety onto the child. Some parents try to make sure that their "first choice" school's screening is not the first or last in the child's series of screenings, so that the child is familiar with the process but not burned out by it. If it turns out that the child is truly at his or her worst because of an illness or for some other reason, the parent should inform the school. If a child's screening does not line up with the written evaluations of preschool teachers, the school may even follow up on its own to ensure that the child wasn't observed on an "off" day.

If you are seeking admission to a middle school, the school tour and interview process will more directly involve your child, who, after all, has spent a few years in school already accumulating an academic record and other accomplishments and talents as well as forming an opinion on what a school should be like. Your child will probably be tested and may be invited to schedule a full day visit to the school. Some schools will accept standardized test results in lieu of sitting for an exam, especially for families relocating from a great distance. Middle school applicants are also usually expected to complete various essay questions on applications and attend an interview. Your child's enthusiasm about the school (or indifference) will undoubtedly show through at the interview and visit. It's an individual decision how far to go in preparation and coaching—the process is stressful enough already and you certainly don't want your naturally ebullient 5th grader coming off as a robot. However, depending upon your child, a few gentle reminders about eye contact and handshakes may be in order. Not leaving this to chance, at least one private elementary school in the area incorporates "interviewing skills" into its 4th grade communications curriculum for the purpose of preparing for middle school interviews.

In parent interviews, you may be asked about your family, your child's strengths and weaknesses, and the reason for your interest in the school. In the hopes of making a good first impression, some parents are so afraid to offend that they simply sit there grinning and gushing indiscriminately about the school and their child. (One parent related how he and his wife turned this scenario into a more informative process by doing a little probing of their own during the interview to determine if the school was indeed the right place for their daughter. The child was admitted to several schools and the parents felt more confident eliminating a popular school from their list of choices because they used the process to learn more about the school, the lesson here being that just because a school is tremendously popular and admission of your child would make you feel proud doesn't mean that the school is right for your child.) It is worth noting that when asked what kind of child the school best serves, many schools replied that they best serve families who support the school's philosophy and teaching style. If the school is truly your "first choice," this would be the time to let the school know, but be sure to explain your reasons. Enough unscrupulous parents have made that claim to multiple schools to make it almost a meaningless designation. (And schools have ways of finding out whether you have designated several "first choices.")

COSTS AND FINANCIAL AID

The schools included in this book were asked to provide tuition figures for the current and upcoming academic year (to the extent available), and availability of tuition payment plans and financial aid. (Additional fees for extended care and after-school programs are covered in a separate section.) Expect frequent, if not annual, tuition increases over the time your child attends private school. While it may seem that there are plenty of Silicon Valley families who can afford not only the tuition but could also underwrite a building project, many more families in the area are already stretched by the high costs of housing and transportation. Add to that a couple of private school tuitions and the financial impact can be significant. Despite this, more than one admission director remarked that many families, for various reasons, are reluctant to apply for financial aid; many schools would like to encourage more to do so. While some families view it as an invasion of their financial privacy and fear potential harm to their child's prospects for admission, schools claim that they keep the financial review process separate from admission decisions. (Most independent schools use the School and Student Service for Financial Aid (SSS) form, which is processed in Princeton, N.J., and results in a computation of the family's eligibility level. Some schools will take into account other factors particular to the unusually high cost of living in this area.) Financial aid of some sort is available from a majority of the schools profiled, although full tuition grants are relatively rare. Financial awards are almost always need-based, confidential, and determined separately from the admissions process. It is fairly rare at the primary and middle school level to find awards based on academic, athletic, or other merit. Awards normally continue year to year so long as financial need continues.

Catholic parochial schools most often have separate tuition figures for members of their own parish (some have a different rate for members who participate in the parish and those who don't), members of other parishes (again, sometimes participating or non-), and non-Catholics. Catholic parochial schools also normally offer substantial (20%-50%) discounts for siblings, and often cap the amount one family can pay at the tuition set for three children (thus, if you have four, you only pay the rate for three). These discounts and caps don't always apply to out-of-parish Catholics or non-Catholics. You can expect a somewhat lower annual tuition increase at parochial schools than at independent schools.

PROGRAM AND PHILOSOPHY

We asked each school to provide its "Mission Statement" or Goals, and to describe its academic program and philosophy. These statements are included verbatim, in quotes. It is important that parents understand and support the philosophy of their child's school, and it is equally important that they understand and support the school's teaching methods.

In the early 1990's, considerable debate and controversy ensued over the methods used for teaching reading and, to a lesser extent, math. The reading debate pitted the "whole language" approach (which encourages children to pick up word clues from pictures and to use inventive spelling) against phonics (which asks the child to sound out words). Currently, it is most common to find programs that use some combination of the two methods or a "multi-sensory" approach to accommodate different learning styles.

At issue in math instruction is "concept-based math" which emphasizes problem solving and "real-life" application of math over rote memorization of rules and repetitive exercises. Again, the trend seems to be to move away from the extremes toward a balanced approach that uses manipulatives (especially in the kindergarten and early primary grades) and application skills but still teaches straightforward "math facts."

In this section we also asked for descriptions of other subject matter offerings, including music, art and foreign languages, and for information about any unique or special programs at the school (e.g. outdoor education and overnight field trips). Foreign language options are usually narrow at the primary grade level, so if your child must learn French, for example, you may only have a few schools to choose from.

We also asked the schools to describe their approach to computer training and use. In some schools, due to budget constraints or different priorities, you may find no more than a few computers and no integration of computer use with the curriculum. Many schools, however, are devoting considerable resources to up-to-date technology and computer training. We found many schools providing separate computer labs, often equipped with rows of i-Macs and staffed with a full-time computer instructor (who often trains the teachers as well as students), student-designed school web sites, Internet access, and the early introduction of keyboarding skills. At the other end of the technology spectrum are those schools that deliberately exclude computers from the classroom for express pedagogical reasons. Parents must decide which approach to technology and computer use they feel most comfortable with.

HOMEWORK

How much is required at each grade level? This has become another hot topic of late, as many parents are questioning the value of the increasing homework load, especially into the middle school years when children are assigned up to three hours an evening on top of after-school sports and other co-curricular activities (not to mention chores and family and social activities). Advocates of homework, especially in the early school years, claim that it helps teach basic time management skills and keeps parents current and involved in their child's education. At the other extreme, some schools have taken the step of eliminating homework altogether, in favor of encouraging families to use their evenings together for family time or reading.

GRADING SYSTEMS

You will see the full range among the schools here—although it is rare to see letter grades (A - F) assigned below the 3rd grade. Most independent schools also provide written evaluations to supplement the "checklist" style report card.

STANDARDIZED TEST SCORES

In recent years there has been an increasing emphasis and focus on test scores in our public schools. In the spring, when the California public school standardized test results are released to the media and later to parents and teachers, we are all advised of the numerous factors that make a good school (and a good student), test scores being just one measure. Nonetheless, the scores do result in a kind of ranking system, inflating (and deflating) egos and real estate values in their wake. In 1999 the state initiated the "Academic Performance Index," which actually does rank public schools on the basis of the school's overall performance on standardized testing in comparison to other schools with similar demographic characteristics. Information on it and other ways the state assesses public schools can be found at www.cde.ca.gov.

Unlike in public schools, standardized testing is not required in private schools, nor do the private schools administer the same test, preventing (for better or worse) an apples-to-apples comparison of private versus public school performance. Private schools do not ordinarily release their scores to the public either, other than to issue a generalized statement in a school catalog or parent newsletter along the lines of how their students compare overall to a national or state average of public or private school students (especially when they compare favorably). Others will share that information only with parents of their own students. Since test scores are only one measure of a school's performance, many schools are reluctant to issue data that they feel may be misconstrued by anxious, test-focused parents. Many are concerned that teaching children to perform well on multiple choice tests comes at the expense of encouraging critical thinking and creativity. If you are concerned about testing, you should ask the schools, but be prepared for some carefully worded disclaimers about the limited value of standardized test scores.

MIDDLE AND HIGH SCHOOL ATTENDANCE

We asked which middle schools and high schools the schools' graduates enter upon graduation. Some patterns are clear: many of the Catholic parochial school students go on to Catholic high schools, for example, and students from the selective independent day schools seem to get distributed among the selective middle and high schools. Does your choice of private elementary school determine the outcome? According to a placement counselor at one of these schools, there is not a feeder school system whereby graduates of certain schools are virtually guaranteed admission to the secondary school of their choice. Due to intense competition for space, attending a certain elementary school does not guarantee admission to a chosen middle or high school, as some of these schools attempt to balance their entering classes with excellent students from a number of schools (including public).

ATHLETICS

The emphasis on sports, and the caliber of the sports facilities varies tremendously among the schools. Some schools have a separate physical education instructor, some have programs that emphasize "lifetime sports" or cooperative games, and some have access to wonderful facilities such as swimming pools, athletic fields and fully equipped gymnasiums. Others may simply have the teacher take the children outside on the courtyard every other day for a game of kickball. Competitive, inter-scholastic athletics, usually in one of the private school leagues, does not start until 5th grade.

FACULTY

We asked for basic demographic data about the teachers: gender, educational training, credentials and ethnicity. We also inquired about the faculty selection process and how the schools keep their teachers current and qualified. Note that private schools are not required to hire credentialed teachers though many do. A California teaching credential requires a bachelor's degree, one year of specialized training, student teaching, and a passing score on the CBEST exam and a criminal background check. (California public schools require credentials for teachers, though thousands are teaching on "emergency credentials" because of a teacher shortage.) The CBEST exam has been criticized for being too easy (some say it tests to the 6th grade level) and for being culturally biased.

Some people feel that no teacher should be able to teach without a credential; others feel that people with a high level of expertise in a particular field do not necessarily need a credential to have the skills to teach. Private schools are allowed to make their own decisions in this regard—to hire a Ph.D. in biology to teach biology absent a credential, or to require all teachers hold credentials.

Among the Catholic schools, the qualifications for faculty are set by the governing diocese or archdiocese. The San Francisco Archdiocese, for example, requires that all teachers have bachelor's degrees, but they need not have a current teaching credential to be considered for hiring. The individual schools may set that policy if they wish. In a recent survey, approximately one-third of teachers in the Archdiocese had master's degrees and approximately two-thirds had current California teaching credentials. An additional number of teachers had out-of-state credentials from states with which California has reciprocity. Private schools also set their own policies in the area of teacher continuing education. Few will dispute that teachers who are current in their fields make better teachers. Teachers stay current through teacher in-service days (those days when there is no school), professional activities such as conferences, and, sometimes, sabbaticals. Teachers in Catholic schools have salary incentives that reward in-service training, though no minimum hours are required. (Religion teachers, however, must be separately certified and participate in 40 hours of in-service every four years.)

State laws have become stricter in recent years with regard to criminal background checks of employees of public and private schools (following the 1997 on-campus murder of a public high school student allegedly by a school employee). Bay Area newspapers have reported two arrests in the past few years of employees at Bay Area private schools for alleged sexual crimes. In the past, a private school was required to submit the fingerprints of a new unlicensed employee (credentialed teachers have background checks as part of the credentialing process) to the Department of Justice for a background check, but could do it upon hiring the person. The criminal check could take months to complete. Now, the person seeking employment must obtain the background check and produce it to the school as a condition of employment. Since 1997, private schools may not hire an unlicensed person until he or she has produced a background clearance, nor may private schools any longer "emplo[y] a person who has been convicted of a violent or serious felony." (Education Code, Section 44237 et seq.)

CAMPUS

This section is intended to give a snapshot of the school and its amenities, from the elements that shape daily life on campus, such as its facilities, meal service, and uniform requirements to the programs that affect parents such as parent participation and fundraising programs.

DRUGS/ALCOHOL/DISCIPLINE

We also asked schools about their policies regarding discipline and drug and alcohol use and abuse prevention. Most schools have a written policy of some sort, usually more fully outlined in the parent/student handbook. Most schools also typically have some kind of education program, often incorporated into the health and physical education curriculum, or in religious schools, in the religious curriculum.

LEARNING DIFFERENCES/DISABILITIES

We asked the schools to describe their student support services including services for children with learning differences and disabilities. (A majority of schools offer none other than referral.) Learning differences or disabilities that interfere with a child's ability to learn or require an adjustment of teaching styles for a child to best learn are often discovered in the early grades. Such a discovery can be traumatic for parents who have done "all the right things" to make sure their child has advantages in life. Parents need to know that this is not an uncommon situation and that plenty of children progress through the grades quite normally and happily even with mild learning disabilities (some with tutoring, modification of teaching methods and testing, etc.). Children who have more serious learning disabilities can find specific resources through private sources or through the public school districts, which are required to provide services to all children in their districts. Second opinions should be obtained (pediatricians can provide referrals). A good resource for information on learning disabilities is the Schwab Foundation for Learning in San Mateo at www.schwablearning.org, or (650) 655-2410.

PARENT PARTICIPATION AND FUNDRAISING

The schools vary widely in their expectations of parent participation—some openly encourage parent participation in the classroom and elsewhere, others would prefer to limit parent participation to field trip driving and fundraising. Some schools set a minimum number of hours each family must volunteer, others leave it to personal choice. At most schools, fundraising is an important and time-consuming activity. Even with annual tuition increases, most schools experience a "gap" between operating costs and tuition income, and have goals for supporting their financial aid programs and, perhaps, funding capital improvements on their campuses. It can be informative to review the annual reports of the schools you are interested in—you'll get a sense of the school's financial health and the breadth of parental, alumni, and even faculty support (not to mention the range of donation amounts). A high percentage of participation by parents should be viewed as a positive sign, indicating broad support for the school, confidence in its administrators, and a desire of these families to provide the best education possible for their children and their classmates. Fundraising also may involve a major annual event, such as an auction or party, which the parents are expected to plan, attend, and support in some way. Finally, many schools participate in scrip programs and gift-wrap sales to raise additional cash.

EXTENDED DAY AND AFTER-SCHOOL PROGRAMS

With the exception of the schools that are only middle schools or middle/high combinations, most schools have an extended day program, some with coverage beginning as early as 6:30 a.m. and extending as late as 6:30 p.m. Almost all programs are at an additional cost. Some will allow drop-in use (good for parents who only have the occasional need for after-school care), and some (but not many) offer programs during school breaks (helpful for working parents who can't take off from work or find other child care during those times). The character and quality of the after-school programs varies from school to school, depending to a great extent on the staff and facilities available to the children. If you plan to enroll your child in the after-school program, be sure to visit it on your tour (or try to schedule a separate visit when it is in session, if it is not open during the regular school tour). If you are looking at middle schools, take note that while none of them have separate "extended care" programs, students at many of these schools are allowed to stay on campus after school to participate in after-school activities or to use the library. At K-8 schools, the students may be required to check in with the school's program.

FINAL WORDS

At the conclusion of the questionnaire, we posed two questions designed to allow the school to describe its unique attributes: What sets the school apart from others, and how do parents and students characterize the school? The school's perception of itself can be informative. If the school claims that it's known for its strong spiritual environment and this is a low priority for you, for example, it may not be a good fit. In addition to reading the comments of parents and students here, it is always a good idea to talk to parents in the school (they often help run the tours) and to parents of recent graduates (who may be more candid, especially on the subject of making the transition out of the school and into middle school or high school).

THE PUBLIC SCHOOL ALTERNATIVE

It is not our intent to steer people away from public schools. Clearly, California's public schools have been the focus of a lot of criticism over the past years, much of it deserved. However, some positive changes have occurred in recent years due to reduced class sizes in the lower grades, superhuman effort by some excellent teachers and administrators, and community support such as the passage of local bond measures and the financial support of foundations to supplement school budgets. Good public schools are out there, some every bit as good if not better than some of the schools in this guide. Information on public schools can be obtained from the school district (ask for the school report card, which they are required to produce), from the Department of Education in Sacramento (www.cde.ca.gov), and from various web sites.

Checklist: What to Look for in a School
K-8

Who runs the school? A board? One person? Do parents have input?

What is the class size? Is there one class per grade or more?

What is the teaching style? Are children expected to sit at desks in rows, or is it set up for more activity?

What qualifications do teachers have?

What sort of student does the school seek to produce after nine years? (All schools will say students who are curious and have a love of learning, but what does the school emphasize? Test-taking? Creativity? Independence?)

Does the school appear to have the diversity you seek (student body, administration/faculty)?

Does the school teach what you want your child to learn?

Look at the children's work on the walls of the classrooms and see if it is consistent with your expectations.

Does the school offer activities that interest your child?

Ask how well students score on standardized tests (some schools will show you test results, most will give you an average).

If you will use the extended care program, does it meet your expectations? (Do you want your child to rest after an active day at school, do all of her homework, or take enrichment classes?)

    - Are the enrichment classes taught by qualified instructors?

Does the school have adequate and safe outdoor facilities?

What is the school's approach to sports? Competitive or non?

Is the school accredited? By whom? If not, has it sought accreditation?

If your child ends up being identified as having a learning disability or difference, what resources does the school have to assist your child in learning?

Does the school "track" students (i.e., put them in ability groups)? (If the school does track, how do they prevent students in the low groups from feeling inadequate?)

What percentage of students are functioning at grade level?

What does the school offer in terms of music, art, foreign languages?

When you visit, do the students seem happy to be there? Are they well-behaved and courteous? Do the teachers seem nurturing and caring toward the students? Do the teachers seem to have control over the classroom and the students' attention?

Does this seem to you to be a place where your child would be happy and learning?

Does this seem a place where you would feel comfortable as a parent?

ADDITIONAL CONCERNS WHEN EVALUATING A MIDDLE SCHOOL

Would your child be better served by attending middle school at a K-8 school or at a 6-12 school (i.e., being among the oldest and the leaders in a school, or the youngest in a school)? In a school that is 6-12, middle school students have access to more sophisticated facilities and equipment, such as science labs, theaters, etc. But they are also exposed earlier to "high school behavior."

In middle school, certain classes should be taught by teachers with a speciality (preferably a degree in the specific subject area): math, science, English, foreign language, P.E.

What programs does the school have for students who are above or below grade level? (You want your child to be challenged, and to have access to extra help if needed.)

If your child has a specific interest or talent, does the school have the ability/ motivation and facilities to help develop it?

This is the age when students (often without knowing the ramifications) begin to imitate behavior and language they see/hear in the media. What does the school do to help teach children proper language, behavior and respect for others?

What does the school do to deter drug and alcohol use?

Does the school sponsor social events for middle school students such as dances?

Does the school have any support systems for students (and parents) regarding the challenges specific to this age group?

Are the classrooms sufficiently spacious for this larger-sized (and sometimes rowdier and hormone-driven) age group?

Does the school have adequate facilities for science experiments?

What more advanced computer technology is available to this age group?

  -How is Internet access monitored?

How do the 8th graders do on the high school admission tests? (Average score/ percentile)

What high schools did last year's graduates attend? What help does the school offer in preparing students for the high school admission process?

Can the school provide a safe and secure environment for your child until the time you are able to pick him up?

Other areas that are important to you:

_____

_____

_____

_____

_____

_____

_____

THE CAREY SCHOOL

One Carey School Lane
San Mateo, CA 94403
(650) 345-8205 *fax (650) 345-2528*
www.careyschool.com

Robert W. Simpson, *Head of School*

We are looking for "a child who can be happy here, a child who can succeed in this very particular environment and a child who: (1) can operate well above the norm and (2) whose academic needs we feel we can meet." **Our school best serves** "a child who can absorb what the school offers, who can have a good time and who can be an active and contributing member of the Carey community. We work best with parents who agree with and support the school's philosophy."

GENERAL

Co-ed PreK-5th grade day school. Nonsectarian. Founded by James and Mary Carey in 1928. **Nonprofit**, member of CAIS. **Accreditation:** CAIS. **Enrollment:** Approximately 185. **Average class size:** N/P. **Length of school year:** 175. **Length of school day:** 8:30 a.m.-12:30 p.m. (preschool), 8:30 a.m.-2 p.m. (K), 8:30 a.m.-3 p.m. (grades 1-5). **Location:** In the city of San Mateo, near Alameda de las Pulgas and Highway 92.

STUDENT BODY

Geographic: The majority of families live in San Mateo, Burlingame, Belmont and Hillsborough, respectively. Some students come from San Carlos, Half Moon Bay and other nearby communities. **Ethnicity:** N/P. **Foreign students (I-20 status):** N/P. **Two f/t working/single parent families:** N/P.

ADMISSION

<u>PreK & Kindergarten</u>. **Application deadline:** Early February (check with school). **Age requirement:** Age 4 by September 1 (PreK), 5 by September 1 (K). **Application fee:** $110. **Application process:** Schedule appointment to meet with school administration and tour campus. Appointment is prerequisite to formal application to school. PreK and K screenings take place on scheduled Saturday mornings and include a question-and-answer period for the parents and a teacher-child period without the parents. The head of school then contacts parents to schedule a follow-up student visit. Formal classroom observations for parents of applicants at all grade levels take place by appointment. Informal coffees are held in late February to introduce prospective parents to parents of current Carey School students. Prospective parents are also invited to curriculum night, in early February, and an open house, in early March. **Preschools visited by admission**

director: N/P. **Number of applications received:** N/P. ("Number exceeds spaces available.") **Number of spaces in last year's K class filled by school's own preschool grads:** 18. **Preferences:** Siblings, if qualified. **Other grades**. **Application deadline:** Same deadlines as Pre-K and K. **Application process:** Grade-school applicants undergo standardized testing and the completion of some teacher-assigned materials. The head of school contacts parents to set up an appointment for a student visit. **Admission test:** N/P. **Test score/GPA cut-off:** N/P. **Number of openings in grades 1-5:** N/P (sometimes a few spaces do become available, strength of applicant is a consideration).

COSTS

Latest tuition: $7,630 (PreK), $9,200 (K), $9,530 (grades 1-4), $9,770 (grade 5). **Last tuition increase:** N/P. **Tuition payment plan:** 2- and 8-payment plans available. **Sibling discount:** N/P. **Percentage of students receiving financial aid:** Approximately 6%. Tuition assistance is provided to students who qualify in one of two categories: (1) A scholarship assistance program to attract and retain students of superior academic ability, and (2) A tuition aid program which first supports families who may be under-represented in the school's demographics and then offers assistance to otherwise qualified tuition assistance applicants. The school encourages families to apply for tuition assistance. **Average grant award:** N/P. **Number of full/partial tuition grants:** N/P.

PROGRAM AND PHILOSOPHY

School's mission statement. "The mission of The Carey School is to provide a safe learning environment where students of a diverse population develop and foster a life-long love of learning. [Goals:] To provide opportunities for student involvement and experiences in accepting responsibility and self-direction. To provide a strong and challenging academic focus which emphasizes development of basic skills and exploration within a context of respect for individual differences in interests, abilities, needs and learning styles. To provide a safe and supportive teaching and learning environment. To increase an awareness of the value of learning. To improve the performance of all students in reading, writing, speaking, listening, calculating, study skills and critical thinking. To promote the values of kindness, integrity and tolerance and respect for people. To uphold the value of self-discipline. To enhance the ability to resolve conflicts." **Academic program.** **Approach to teaching reading:** Combination of whole language and phonics. **Approach to teaching math:** "Concepts, computation and application." **Approach to technology and computer training:** Full-time computer teacher. Technology plan is project-based. Keyboarding integrated into curriculum in 2nd grade. Computers on campus are networked. Teachers are encouraged to attend off-site computer training at school's expense. **Other courses/offerings:** Both Spanish and French are taught in Pre-K and K; student chooses one foreign language to study in grades 1-5. Foreign languages, art, music, computer, P.E., library, art and science are taught by specialists. **Special programs:**

Outdoor education in 5th grade with field trip. Drama and creative arts studies and activities are offered in conjunction with library program. **Average nightly homework:** In grades K-5, may range from 10 minutes in Kindergarten to 1.5 hours (4 nights/week) in 5th grade. **Grading system:** "Narrative and symbols." **Frequency of parent/teacher conferences:** Twice/year. Teachers also available by e-mail. **Standardized test scores:** Provided to parents (child's scores only). **High schools attended by recent graduates:** Include Woodside Priory, St. Joseph's, Menlo, Castilleja, Crystal Springs. **Other indicators that the school is accomplishing its goals:** "All students participate in various community service programs."

ATHLETICS

Physical education program: N/P. **Interscholastic athletics:** 5th graders may participate in a year-long co-ed basketball clinic.

FACULTY

Gender: Approximately 80% female, 20% male. **Ethnicity:** N/P. **Highest educational degree earned:** All have Bachelor's degrees, several have Master's degrees. The school looks for age-appropriate teaching skills in its faculty. **Credentials:** N/P. **Teacher/student ratio:** 1:12. **Faculty training and professional development:** The school reports best results in recruiting faculty through word of mouth and the Internet; it credits success in retaining faculty through the support of ongoing professional development.

EXTENDED CARE/AFTER-SCHOOL PROGRAMS

Extended care (before- and after-school) is available for all grade levels. The morning program begins at 7:30 a.m.; the afternoon program runs until 6 p.m. **Cost:** Additional charge, either paid with tuition or at a higher drop-in daily rate (advance reservation required). **Drop-in:** Available with reservation. **No coverage on:** N/P. **Snacks:** N/P. **Homework:** N/P. **Staff/student ratio:** Approximately 1:12. **After-school classes:** See below.

CAMPUS LIFE

Facilities: The school has been in its current location since 1955. The classrooms are arranged in a U-shaped configuration opening to a central patio. The school is in the process of planning and building updated facilities. **Meals:** Available at an additional cost. **Transportation:** N/P. **Uniforms:** None, dress code calls for "safety and good taste." P.E. uniforms. **Co-curricular activities/clubs:** Offerings have included "After-school Adventures," cooking, karate, Tae Kwon Do, creative writing, model making, and instrumental music. **Student support services:** N/P. **Services for children with learning differences:** None. **Counselor/student ratio:** N/P. **Policies regarding discipline, drug/alcohol use and abuse prevention and AIDS awareness:** Awareness classes. **Summer program:** None.

PARENT PARTICIPATION

Volunteers are used for classroom activities, all-school events, and fundraising. **Parent education:** An evening series is offered in the spring. **Fundraising:** Major fundraising events include the Carey Fest and Auction.

WHAT SETS SCHOOL APART FROM OTHERS?

"Strong academics and sense of community."

HOW DO PARENTS/STUDENTS CHARACTERIZE THE SCHOOL?

"Carey's atmosphere was that of a family. During eight years at Carey, my teachers were eager to help and support me. Students were friendly and open-minded with each other. At Carey, I felt safe and free to share my ideas and opinions. I will always remember the Carey School, for it prepared me for the rigors of high school and more importantly helped me to become a better person."

"It is almost impossible not to have fun at Carey. Teachers make classroom learning interesting. Outdoor fun, on three playgrounds, gives students plenty of room for almost any type of game, activity or sport. My years at Carey, all seven of them, have been filled with fun."

CASTILLEJA SCHOOL

1310 Bryant Street
Palo Alto, CA 94301
(650) 328-3160 *fax (650) 326-8036*
Info@castilleja.org
www.castilleja.org

Joan Lonergan, *Head of School*
Anne Cameron, *Middle School Head*
Jill Lee, *Director of Admission and Financial Aid*

We are looking for "self-motivated, enthusiastic learners who will both contribute to and benefit from our community." **Our school best serves** "curious, motivated students who possess an eagerness to learn and an understanding of the advantages of a single sex educational environment."

GENERAL

Girls' day middle school and high school. Nonsectarian. Founded 1907. **Nonprofit,** member of CAIS, NAIS, BAIHS. **Accreditation**: WASC (6-year term through 2003). **Enrollment**: 385. **Average class size**: 15 (in middle school). **Length of school year**: 9-month calendar. **Length of school day:** 8 a.m.-3:15 p.m. (clubs take place during school day, sports after school). **Location:** In a residential area of Palo Alto, near Stanford University (Embarcadero Road exit from Highway 101).

STUDENT BODY

Geographic: Most students come from towns in Santa Clara and San Mateo Counties. **Ethnicity:** 68% Caucasian (non-Latina), 18% Asian/Pacific Islander, 6% Middle Eastern or East Indian, 5% African-American, 3% Latina. **Foreign students (I-20 status):** None. **Two f/t working parent families:** 60% (includes full- and part-time). **Single parent families:** 1%.

ADMISSION

Application deadline: Mid-January. **Application fee:** $50. **Application process:** Student and parent questionnaires, teacher recommendations, standardized testing, transcripts and on-campus interviews. The school advises prospective applicants to review the admission package for further details. **Admission test:** N/P. **Number of applications received:** 180 applications received last year for 60 spaces. (Openings in grades 7 and 8 occur "as space is available.") **Test score/GPA cut-off:** None, though typically, most admitted students have earned primarily A's and B's. **Preferences:** "We value the relationship we have developed with current families, and, to that end, siblings are given special consideration in the admission process. As with all applicants, the sibling candidate must be a strong student and good citizen in order to gain admission to Castilleja."

COSTS

Latest tuition: $16,550 + $725 for required meal program = $17,275. **Last tuition increase:** 5.5%. **Tuition payment plan:** Available. **Sibling discount:** None. **Percentage of students receiving financial aid:** 13%. **Average grant award:** $8,500. **Number of full tuition grants**: "Varies." **Percentage of partial tuition grants that are half-tuition or more:** 61%. **Other information regarding financial assistance:** Admission decisions are made regardless of a family's financial need. The school is approaching the end of a $12 million capital campaign.

PROGRAMS AND PHILOSOPHY

School's mission statement/goals. "Castilleja School educates young women by fostering their intellectual, physical, creative and emotional growth through an exemplary college preparatory experience within a diverse and supportive community. By blending tradition with thoughtful innovation, the curriculum encourages both individual achievement and collaborative learning. Castilleja's comprehensive program promotes the development of character, compassion, curiosity, and the capacity for effective leadership." **Statement of philosophy.** "Castilleja's philosophy is shaped by both tradition and current research that affirm the academic and personal advantages of girls' schools. We demonstrate this conviction in the conscious attention we pay to the needs, issues, pedagogies and opportunities particular to girls. While our emphasis is on the development of the intellect, Castilleja is committed to the education of the whole person: heart, body and spirit as well as mind. Castilleja is committed to excellence. We believe in small classes led by dedicated teachers who exhibit strong academic preparation, enthusiasm for teaching and learning, and concern for each student. We value a curriculum that blends traditional teaching with thoughtful innovation, and we applaud both individual achievement and successful collaboration. We expect students to master information, use technology effectively, and develop the critical thinking skills that support lifelong learning. Castilleja recognizes the importance of parents who are involved with their daughters' education and encourages them to work in partnership with the school. Castilleja fosters leadership in the classroom and through a wide assortment of extracurricular offerings, including team sports, clubs, community service projects, student government, dramatic and musical performance, art and science exhibits and service-learning. We recognize each student's individuality and help her excel in her unique interests. Castilleja expects its student to participate as citizens of a small school and a larger world. We promote, through experience and example, the development of self-confidence and concern for others, and the capacity for responsible risk-taking and ethical decision-making. Conscience, Courtesy, Character, Courage, and Charity—Castilleja's Five C's, which date back to the school's founding headmistress—still resonate, reminding students that personal values must accompany academic achievement. Castilleja prepares its graduates to succeed at the most competitive colleges in the nation and to pursue lives committed to personal fulfillment, social responsibility and leadership." **Academic program.** "Castilleja's academic program is college preparatory in nature, designed to be intrinsically enjoyable and to help students make informed choices about their future roles in society. The school's pedagogical approaches and course offerings are informed by research findings that focus on the distinctive ways in which girls learn. The educational program combines the tradition of academic excellence with educational innovation, strong individual achievement with an emphasis on team-building, a knowledge of Western culture within a global awareness, and the development of self-confidence with compassion for other human beings." **Approach to teaching math/reading:** N/P (middle school). **Approach to technology and computer training:** "Technology is an integral part of a Castilleja education. Computers are located in both labs and regular classrooms and are fully equipped with high-speed Internet access, state-of-the-art programs and networking capabilities. Teachers will often collaborate with a designated technology faculty member and instruct students within the context of a core subject's curriculum. Students have unrestricted access to the school computers during school hours and also after school in the library until 7 p.m. **Other courses/offerings:** Foreign languages (French, Japanese, Latin and Spanish), fine and performing arts, middle school student government, and other clubs. Students also participate in overnight retreats and the school's service-learning (community service) program. **Average nightly homework:** N/P. **Frequency of parent/teacher conferences:** Middle School parent-teacher conferences are held annually (during the 1st semester). **Grading system:** The school sends out grades on a quarterly basis. First and 3rd quarter grades are accompanied by comment cards for every student from every teacher. These narratives are the essential means of evaluating students. Progress reports are used to inform parents of dramatic shifts in a student's academic performance. Faculty advisors are also an important contact person for parents. **Standardized test scores:** N/P. **High schools attended by recent graduates:** N/P. (Castilleja is grades 6-12.) **Other indicators that the school is accomplishing its goals:** "Our commitment to providing opportunities for students to do their best work and be their best selves manifests itself not only through our course offerings but also in this environment of small classes and close teacher-student relations. Ours is a real community, where teachers come to know their students as individuals both in the classroom and out. It is an atmosphere that fosters respect for learning and encourages challenges, where students know they will find the support and resources they need for both academic and extracurricular risk-taking."

ATHLETICS

Physical education program: The school's goal is "to offer a sequential age-appropriate curriculum to allow girls to develop a lifelong commitment to physical well-being, health and personal fitness." **Interscholastic athletics:** Middle school students participate in after-school sports including swimming, softball, soccer, basketball, volleyball and tennis.

FACULTY

Gender: N/P. **Ethnicity:** Approx. 85% Caucasian (non-Latino), 7% Asian (includes Filipino), 6% Latino, 2% African-American. 9% of the faculty members are from "international backgrounds." **Highest educational degree earned:** N/P. **Credentials:** N/P. **Teacher/student ratio:** N/P. **Faculty selection and professional development:** "Once it is determined that an opening will occur, the appropriate faculty and administrators review the needs of the school including future curricular developments, educational background and teaching experience of the candidate. Prospective faculty members are solicited through national search organizations and other school contacts. The interview process involves teaching a sample lesson, campus tour, observing a class and interviewing with the academic dean, middle school head and the department head. All faculty members undergo formal reviews on a regular basis." [Professional development:] "Castilleja encourages professional growth by making available funding for national conferences, advanced courses, summer stipends and the like. The school also sponsors bi-annual in-service days which consist of a nationally regarded educational expert working with all faculty for a day or attending several seminars at the California Association of Independent Schools conference."

EXTENDED CARE/AFTER-SCHOOL PROGRAMS

N/P.

CAMPUS LIFE

Facilities: The school is housed in a circa 1910 building and four buildings surrounding a spacious circular courtyard. The campus includes a swimming pool, gymnasium and an athletic field. A former residence hall has been renovated and now houses a student center, library, dining facilities, foreign language classrooms, a language lab, senior lounge, multimedia and training labs, faculty center and offices. The campus also includes two art studios and a gallery, a dance studio and a theater. Construction completed in 1997 includes complete renovation of the science wing and the creation of new middle school facilities which include six classrooms, a student lounge, meeting rooms and middle school office space. The school's newly remodeled Arrillaga Family Campus has three computer labs, "including a high-performance Graphics Lab with three Sun SPARCstations and eight Silicon Graphics Indys, as well as multimedia and training labs with 38 Macs and PowerPCs. The network includes a fiber optic backbone and high-end Cisco Systems switches that allow 200 to 400MBs of backbone speed between buildings. The school uses a high-speed DSL line to connect its 300-node network to the Internet." The school has two Apple computer labs, a Unix-based multimedia lab, a library study lab and a drop-in study lab. The school uses both Apple Share and Novell servers to support its users. The Espinosa Library/Media Center includes a 12,000 volume automated library, electronic databases, Internet access from all workstations and study space for students. **Meals:** A full lunch and snack program is mandatory and was developed with a nutritionist. **Transportation:** Van service to and from the Palo Alto University Avenue CalTrain station. Carpool lists are made available to the parent body. Some parents have contracted a van service in certain residential areas, although the school does not take responsibility for the service. **Uniforms:** White or navy blue collared shirt (polo shirt, for example), or red Castilleja sweatshirt with uniform light blue skirt or navy blue pants (no jeans or sweat pant material), uniform shorts. Dress white uniform for traditional or formal occasions. **Co-curricular activities/clubs:** More than 30 clubs, including Mochuelo (literary magazine), Counterpoint (newspaper), Paintbrush (yearbook), Student Nation Club, Current Affairs, Art Club, A Capella Singers, and Drama Club. **Student support services:** The school has a part-time licensed clinical social worker available to students for group and individual confidential sessions. All students meet weekly with a faculty advisor in groups of 8-10 students. Advisors monitor the social and academic progress of their advisees, explain school policies, discuss community issues, assist in course selection, serve as a resource, and provide support. Freshmen have a junior peer advisor, and sophomores have a senior peer advisor who co-facilitates the group. Every grade participates in annual retreats focusing on themes and skills that foster age-appropriate growth and group strength. Castilleja offers an academic counseling program to assist students in the planning of their academic programs—the goal of the entire process being to ensure that the student has a course load that will best meet her needs and the school's demands. Castilleja offers peer tutoring to assist students in academic need as well as to provide leadership opportunities for the student body. **Services for students with learning differences:** No formal program. **Counselor/student ratio (not including college counselor):** 2.5:160. One full-time counselor, one counseling intern and one middle school head for students in grades 6-8. **Policies regarding discipline, drug/alcohol use and abuse prevention and AIDS awareness:** "If a student is concerned about her own drug or alcohol use, or the drug or alcohol use of a peer, the response will not be punitive. Students may seek help from the counselor or the Dean of Students. These issues are addressed within the Human Development Department as part of the broader concept of health and wellness. The department's goal is to offer courses that contribute to the development of emotional literacy and resiliency in Castilleja students. Resources are available through the school counselor." **Summer programs:** Castilleja has an 8-week summer camp program for girls completing grades 1-6. Castilleja also participates with 5 other independent schools on the Peninsula in providing a full-scholarship Summer Bridge Program for girls completing grades 4-7 in East Palo Alto and Redwood City public schools.

PARENT PARTICIPATION

A "high percentage" of parents volunteer their time and financial support. **Parent education:** Parent forums are offered throughout the year. **Fundraising:** Major events held in the recent past include a golf tournament, dinners, auctions, and an ongoing Annual Fund program. There is an expectation that every family will contribute at some level.

WHAT SETS SCHOOL APART FROM OTHERS?

"Academic excellence and a focus on leadership development both in and out of the classroom are all within the context of an all-girls educational environment, an essential distinction from other [area] schools ...."

HOW PARENTS/STUDENTS CHARACTERIZE THE SCHOOL?

Parent response(s): "We realize that it is no small undertaking to evaluate the progress of many students, the faculty does so with obvious care and a concern for the wholeness of the student. This just confirms our belief that education at Castilleja extends beyond the dynamism of the classroom into those many other formal and informal opportunities when students interact with faculty and staff members. The girls are very fortunate, and we, as parents, remain grateful."
Student response(s): "It is a friendly environment where students are able to express their thoughts and feelings freely without having to worry about whether they're right or wrong. Casti creates a strong base for our future. We are free to

express our own opinions, and the teachers enforce our creativity to make us individuals in society. The equality found in this school is far superior to the ones that I know, and the simple fact that we are all different but one at the same time creates trust between everyone. The trust and friendship between all of the students and the teachers creates a great work environment and it makes you feel welcome. You are never an outsider at Castilleja. I feel Castilleja is unique in the fact that we are all able to share our ideas no matter how different they are, and that we are free to be ourselves, and not what others make us to be."

"The teachers are amazing, they aren't only your teachers, they are your friends."

"To me, Castilleja is a school where your classmates are always there to lend an ear and help you with your problems. It is a school where the teachers are always ready to give you extra help if you need it, and truly care that you do well. It is a school that challenges the students to achieve their best, and put their best effort into all tasks. It is a school where individuality is encouraged and accepted. That is how I characterize Castilleja."

CHILDREN'S INTERNATIONAL SCHOOL

4000 Middlefield Road
Suite L-1
Palo Alto, CA 94303
(650) 813-9131 *fax (650) 813-9132*
www.cischool.org

Margaret Hicks, *Director*

GENERAL

Co-ed K-8 day school. Nonsectarian. Founded 1995. **Nonprofit. Accreditation:** N/P. **Enrollment**: 90. **Average class size:** N/P (1:10 teacher student ratio). **Length of school year:** Approximately 252 days (full year). **Length of school day:** 9 a.m.-4 p.m. The campus is open 7:30 a.m.-6 p.m. **Location:** In the southern part of Palo Alto. Accessible from 101, San Antonio Road exit.

STUDENT BODY

Geographic: Most students come from Palo Alto and neighboring cities, including Menlo Park, Los Altos, and Mountain View. **Ethnicity:** N/P. **Foreign students (I-20 status):** N/A. **Two f/t working parent families:** "Most." **Single parent families:** N/P.

ADMISSION

<u>Kindergarten</u>. **Application deadline:** Rolling admissions. **Age requirement:** 4 years, 9 months. **Application fee:** $100. **Application process:** Three-day visit by child, parent interview. **Preschools visited by admission director:** "Local preschools." **Number of applications received:** N/P. **Preferences:** Siblings, children of faculty. <u>Other grades</u>. **Application deadline:** Rolling admissions. **Application fee:** $100. **Application process:** Three-day visit by child, parent interview, report cards and two written recommendations. **Admission test:** None. **Test score/GPA cut-off:** None. **Estimated number of openings in grades other than K each year:** N/P. **"We are looking for ..."** N/P. **"Our school best serves ..."** N/P.

COSTS

Latest tuition: $9,960. **Last tuition increase:** N/P. **Tuition payment plan:** "Available." **Sibling discount:** None. **Financial aid:** N/P.

PROGRAM AND PHILOSOPHY

<u>School's mission statement/goals</u>. "Formalizing the vision of its founders, the mission of the Children's International School is to promote the academic achievement of each child and build a foundation for lifelong development through a process of individualized and self-initiated learning; provide an environment that encourages the intellectual, emotional, physical, social and aesthetic development of each child resulting in confidence, creativity and critical thinking; encourage responsible citizenship in a continually changing world by recognizing and supporting each child as a member of a family, and of his or her local and international communities; contribute to educational innovation by developing programs and sharing information with those who seek to improve the nation's schools. The Children's International School welcomes inquiry about the school from any family interested in supporting and advancing this educational mission." <u>Academic program</u>. "The CIS program is based on the philosophy of individualized and self-directed learning. At the core of the school's philosophy is the belief that children can and must learn to accept responsibility, develop independence, understand the logical consequences of their actions and make decisions that help manage their own learning. Working individually with their teachers, all CIS students help plan their daily and weekly goals. They pursue their interests and assignments at their own pace and order, supplementing their core academics with materials and topics of their own interest. They also participate in evaluating and communicating their own educational progress." Classes are organized in multi-age groups. Developmentally based curriculum. **Approach to teaching reading:** N/P. **Approach to teaching math:** N/P. **Approach to technology and computer training:** "Integrated into curriculum beginning in Kindergarten." Computer lab with Internet access. **Other courses/offerings:** Japanese and Spanish in K-8, Latin in grades 6-8, art, choral music, and "practical

life skills" such as cooking, sewing and weaving. **Special programs:** Outdoor education with camping. **Average nightly homework:** None. **Grading system:** N/P. **Frequency of parent/teacher conferences:** N/P. **Standardized test scores:** N/P. **High schools attended by recent graduates:** (Too new to have this data.) **Other indicators that the school is accomplishing its goals:** N/P.

ATHLETICS

Physical education program: Daily P.E. (No other information provided by school.)

FACULTY

(1:10 teacher/student ratio. No other information provided by school.) According to its web site, CIS has eight full-time teachers, and two part-time language instructors.

EXTENDED CARE PROGRAM

Extended care from 7:30 a.m.-9 a.m. and from 4 p.m.-6 p.m. (included at no additional cost). Full-year calendar and extended care program are "designed to meet the needs of working families." **Cost:** No cost. **Drop-in:** N/P. **No coverage on:** Legal holidays (CIS has 8 holidays per year which correspond with the business calendar). **Snacks:** Provided. **Homework:** N/P. **After-school classes:** Within the Cubberley complex, students may take dance, piano, tai kwan do, and tennis. **Staff/student ratio:** N/P.

CAMPUS LIFE

CIS is in the Cubberley Community Center in southern Palo Alto, on Middlefield Road between San Antonio Road and East Charleston Road. The school has access to approximately 10 acres of tennis courts and playing fields during the school day. Cubberley Center has facilities available to the school on a rental basis, including theater and dance studios. Parent communications include a monthly publication, The Compass.

WHAT SETS THE SCHOOL APART FROM OTHERS?

N/P. [Ed. note: Full year schedule is probably the school's most unique feature.]

HOW DO PARENTS/STUDENTS CHARACTERIZE THE SCHOOL?

Student response: "It's not that we do what we like, it's that we like what we do!"

CRYSTAL SPRINGS UPLANDS SCHOOL

400 Uplands Drive
Hillsborough, CA 94010
(650) 342-4175 *fax (650) 342-7611 (admission), (650) 342-7623 (main office)*
www.csus.com
rbenj@csus.com (admission e-mail)

Richard A. Drew, *Head of School*
Roslyn Benjamin, *Director of Admission (Middle School)*

We are looking for "students who want to participate in the life of the school community. We seek students who will be engaged in class, volunteer in the school, play sports, participate in the arts and reach out to their peers. We also look for families who will become involved in the life of the school and who will support the school's philosophy." **Our school best serves** "students who are curious, creative, and eager to learn more about a variety of subjects. Students and their families should be ready for a challenging and exciting middle school experience."

GENERAL

Co-ed day middle school and high school (grades 6-12). **Nonsectarian.** Founded 1953. **Nonprofit**, member CAIS. **Accreditation**: WASC. **Enrollment**: 350. **Average class size**: 15. **Length of school year**: Approximately 190 days. **Length of school day:** 8:15 a.m.-3:10 p.m. **Location:** In a residential area of Hillsborough, a suburban community approximately 20 miles south of San Francisco.

STUDENT BODY

Geographic: Most students come from communities in the San Mateo County region, including Hillsborough, San Mateo, Burlingame, Menlo Park, Atherton, Portola Valley, Woodside and Belmont. **Ethnicity:** 65.5% Caucasian, 23% Asian or Pacific Islander, 5% Latino, 4% African-American, 2% Middle Eastern or East Indian, 0.5% Filipino. **Foreign students (I-20 status):** None. **Two f/t working parent families:** 50%. **Single parent families:** 10%.

ADMISSION

Application deadline: Approximately January 18. **Application fee:** Approximately $50. **Application process:** Student and parent application, student visit and interview, two teacher recommendations, one counselor/principal recommendation, standardized testing, and transcripts for current year and the previous year. **Number of applications received:** 150 applications received last year for 30 6th grade spaces. Openings in other grades vary by year. **Admission test:** N/P. **Test score/GPA cut-off:** None. **Preferences:** N/P.

COSTS

Latest tuition: $15,650 (+ fees) (tuition includes hot lunches and cold snacks). **Last tuition increase:** 5.9%. **Tuition payment plan:** 10-month plan is available. **Sibling discount:** None. **Percentage of students receiving financial aid:** Approximately 18%. **Average grant award:** $9,700. **Number of full time grants:** 17. **Number of partial tuition grants:** 42.86% of grants were half-tuition or more. **Other information regarding financial assistance:** "We encourage all families to apply for financial assistance if they are concerned about their ability to pay tuition. We are 'need-blind' in the admission process; applying for financial assistance will not impact the admission decision."

PROGRAM AND PHILOSOPHY

School's mission statement/goals. "We believe that students learn best in an environment that promotes learning in diverse ways about a complex world, stimulates intellectual and creative development, nurtures the individual within a community of mutual trust, caring and respect, [and] balances academic and extracurricular interests and accomplishments. We encourage critical thinking and intellectual risk taking, responsibility for one's ideas and actions, personal integrity, ethical awareness, and multicultural understanding, individual leadership and cooperative interaction, [and] respect for one's self and for the views of others. We endeavor to equip students with a spirit of inquiry, a respect for human potential, a sense of responsibility for the environment and to the global community, [and] a feeling of joy in lifelong learning." **Academic program.** Students in grades 6, 7 and 8 take courses in English, history, mathematics and science each year and a foreign language (Latin, French or Spanish) in the 7th and 8th grades. (No foreign languages are offered in the 6th grade so that students may take 6 periods of English a week.) In addition, students take fine arts, health, and P.E. courses each year and computer courses in 6th and 7th grades. Math placement is determined by ability and previous experience rather than by grade. The middle school history program includes two years of Origins of Modern Civilization, followed by U.S. history in 8th grade. The science program covers earth science in 6th grade, life science in 7th grade and physical science in 8th grade. Fine arts courses cover art, drama, movement (grade 6), music (grades 6 and 7) and production and design (grade 8). **Approach to teaching reading/math:** N/P (middle school). **Approach to technology and computer training:** Two computer labs with 35 Power Macs. Eight computers in the Crocker Mansion are also available to students for word processing and Internet access. Classroom computers are networked and have Internet access. All 6th graders receive computer instruction and new 7th graders are given help if needed to "catch up." Middle school students also use computers in other classes. Access is available before and after school and during lunch. **Other courses/offerings** Chorus, instrumental music, ensemble, chamber orchestra and bell choir. All middle school students participate in overnight class retreats at the beginning of the year; 7th graders end the year with a week on Catalina Island studying marine biology, and 8th graders travel to Washington, D.C. **Average nightly homework:** Approximately 30 minutes per subject per night on homework. **Grading system:** Letter grades (A-F). **Frequency of parent/teacher conferences:** Organized advisor/parent/student conferences are held after 1st and 3rd quarters to go over grades and comments. **Standardized test scores:** Students are not tested in school until PSATs and SATs. The school's overall performance is provided on request. **High schools attended by recent graduates:** N/P. (The school includes grades 6-12.) **Other indicators that the school is accomplishing its goals:** "Our students are curious, happy and eager to participate in the life of the school. If they look elsewhere for high school (and we hope they don't), they are almost always accepted."

ATHLETICS

Physical education program: Also known as the "mind/body program," the physical education program "aims to educate students about the positive benefits of exercise, diet, and approach. We hope students will lead active lives and teach lifetime sports." There are three full-time P.E. instructors who also coach, and a dance instructor in addition to the director of athletics. **Interscholastic athletics:** Boys compete in the Independent School Athletic League. Sports include soccer, cross-country, tennis, basketball and baseball. The Girls' Independent School Athletic League sports include volleyball, tennis, cross-country, soccer and basketball.

FACULTY

36 full-time, 13 part-time. **Gender:** 50% male, 50% female. **Ethnicity:** 82% Caucasian (non-Latino), 8% Asian/Pacific Islander, 8% African-American. **Highest educational degree held:** 31 Master's, 6 Doctorates, 2 JDs. **Credentials:** N/P.

Teacher/student ratio: 1:10. **Faculty training and professional development:** Faculty are selected through a search process (search organizations, unsolicited resumes, word of mouth). Potential faculty members are interviewed by the department and administration and teach classes on-site. Teachers remain current with professional development assistance (workshops, school visits, classes), in-service programs, and peer assessment.

EXTENDED CARE/AFTER-SCHOOL PROGRAMS

N/P.

CAMPUS LIFE

Facilities: 10-acre suburban campus on the San Francisco Peninsula midway between Palo Alto and San Francisco. The main building, known as the Crocker Mansion, is an 85-year-old building housing a library, administrative offices and classrooms. Two newer buildings house a 400-seat theater, student center and cafeteria, gym, interactive classrooms, science laboratories, computer labs, and fine arts facilities. The library has 11,250 print volumes, an on-line catalog, 36 periodical subscriptions, seven computers with Internet access, and two study rooms providing study space for 70 students. **Meals:** Hot lunches and cold snacks are provided daily (cost included in tuition). **Transportation:** Sam Trans bus from CalTrain station, and van shuttle along Highway 280 corridor from Los Altos to school, depending upon family interest. **Uniforms:** None; dress code prohibits ripped jeans, t-shirts advertising illegal substances, and baseball hats in theater. **Co-curricular activities/clubs:** Yearbook, Students of Color Club, Spanish Club, Math Club, Futures Problem Solving, middle school newspaper and literary magazine, Key Club, middle school musical, singing and dancing groups, Peer Helpers, and community service. **Student support services:** Advisor assigned to each student; health counselor for personal counseling; teachers readily available. **Services for children with learning differences:** Accommodations are made for students with documented learning differences. **Counselor/student ratio:** 1:350. **Policies regarding discipline, drug/alcohol use and abuse prevention and AIDs awareness:** Three rules of school are: 1) Stay on campus, 2) Abstain from drugs, alcohol and tobacco, 3) Be honest. Middle school students learn about sexuality, HIV/AIDS and related issues in 7th grade and about tobacco, alcohol and other drugs and addictions in 8th grade. **Summer programs:** For entering K-9 students, a 5-week morning and afternoon program costs $700 per half-day program.

PARENT PARTICIPATION

"Encouraged, not required." Parent volunteers work on school committees, help drive on field trips and run major fundraiser. **Parent education:** Formal and informal programs, including orientations, newsletters and presentations. New families are matched with a current family. **Fundraising:** One major event in

February—Mansion Madcap, an auction to benefit a designated program. Over 90% of families contribute to Annual Fund. No minimum contribution required.

WHAT SETS SCHOOL APART FROM OTHERS?

"What sets CSU apart from other good independent schools is the contrast between the way we look and the way we act. We look like a traditional college preparatory school but we act like a small college. Again and again CSU students rave about the relationships they develop with their teachers. We ask a great deal of our students, academically, athletically and extracurricularly, and students respond well to these challenges and then challenge us! Our students are unafraid to be different and are encouraged to take academic risks. Our students thrive in the world 'after CSU' and we think that is in part because they learn so much from the CSU community during their four to seven years here."

HOW DO PARENTS/STUDENTS CHARACTERIZE THE SCHOOL?

Parent response: "My son and daughter both graduated from CSU and what has amazed me is how central the school has remained in their lives. They credit CSU with teaching them how to write and to think for themselves. I cannot imagine a better place for them to have gone to school!"

Student response(s): "Aside from having played a total of thirteen sports seasons in my past six and a half years at CSU, I've been amazed by the other 349 people that I go to school with. Whether their strength be in math or the sciences, or English and history and language, or just ... everything, every student here is a student first. But we are also musicians, actors and actresses, athletes, computer wizards and student leaders."

"Participation in student government has given me the opportunity to experience the amazing support system here. There is a mutual respect between the faculty/administration and the students. All of us students are taught by teachers. That's a given. But what isn't a given is how committed these teachers are to helping us understand and make connections. The commitment to academic excellence isn't just about getting good grades and taking the hardest classes. Teachers here at CSU meet with their students during free periods, study halls, before and after school, and even at lunch, if necessary, to help us out. It's amazing how supportive they are of our activities and interests, even outside the classroom. I see my teachers at games, plays and other events that we participate in. I have grown during my time at CSU in ways that I never thought possible."

FIVE WOUNDS SCHOOL

90 Five Wounds Lane
San Jose, CA 95116
(408) 293-0425 *fax (408) 971-7607*
www.fivewounds.org

Sandra Jewett, *Principal* (Sjewett@fivewounds.org)
Luisa Matos, *Office Manager* (admissions)

We are looking for "families in search of academic excellence and spiritual formation for their children." **Our school best serves** "families who will form a meaningful partnership with our school to ensure the success of our students. We strive to ensure that our children are prepared for the 21st century."

GENERAL

Co-ed K-8 Catholic parochial school (95% of students are Catholic). Founded 1960. **Accreditation**: WASC. **Nonprofit. Enrollment**: 270. **Average class size**: 28. **Length of school year**: Approximately 180 days. **Length of school day**: 8 a.m.-2:45 p.m. **Location:** In the heart of the "Little Portugal" section of San Jose, adjacent to Highway 101.

STUDENT BODY

Geographic: Most students come from San Jose, Santa Clara, Morgan Hill, Gilroy, and Milpitas. **Ethnicity:** 50% Caucasian (non-Latino), 24% Filipino, 17% Latino, 8% Asian/Pacific Islander, 1% African-American. **Foreign students (I-20 status):** None. **Two f/t working parent families:** 90%. **Single parent families:** 10%.

ADMISSION

<u>Kindergarten</u>. **Application deadline:** Mid-August (call school for exact date). **Age requirement:** 5 years old by December 1. **Application fee:** "$340 plus" ($50 of which is non-refundable). **Application process:** A placement test is given to each applicant. The test consists of letter recognition, numbers, shapes, directions, cutting, etc. **Preschools visited by admission director:** N/P. **Number of applications received:** 50 applications received last year for 40 spaces, 15 of the K spaces filled by the preschool students of Dom Dinish Preschool (affiliated with school). **Preferences:** Siblings, parishioners. <u>Other grades</u>. **Application fee and deadline:** Same as K. **Application process/testing:** A placement exam is administered to each applicant. Core proficiencies are tested. Call for test dates. **Test score cut-off:** 80%. **Estimated number of openings in grades other than K each year:** 25.

COSTS

Latest tuition: K: $2,970 for in-parish, $3,400 otherwise. G1-8: $3,300 for in-parish, $3,750 otherwise. **Last tuition increase:** 10%. **Tuition payment plan:** "Available." **Sibling discount:** Substantial. **Financial aid:** 5% of students receive some form of financial aid. **Average grant award:** $400. **Number of full tuition grants:** 5. **Number of partial tuition grants:** Five, all of which were half-tuition or more.

PROGRAM AND PHILOSOPHY

<u>School's mission statement/goals.</u> "To provide a place of spiritual formation and to facilitate student academic excellence and success in a nurturing Catholic Christian environment." [Academic philosophy:] "As Catholic educators, we seek to emulate the teachings of Jesus and to 'teach as Jesus did.' In the midst of a multi-cultural and global society, we acknowledge our responsibility to provide a holistic education for each student in our school. In an atmosphere of Best Teaching Practices and in a student-centered environment, we encourage individual growth through internalization of self-discipline, self-esteem, respect and responsibility as it pertains to life-long learning skills. In partnership with our parents, we strive to together promote academic achievement, and to nurture the spiritual, intellectual, social, physical and psychological potential of each member of our student community." **Academic program. Approach to teaching reading:** "A balanced approach to reading including phonemic awareness and a holistic approach." **Approach to teaching math:** "Balanced approach to math including the use of manipulatives, graphing calculators, etc." **Approach to technology and computer training:** "Computers in every classroom, including a computer lab. The school has a dedicated computer instructor. Computers have Internet access. Networked computers are available in the library for research." **Other courses/offerings** Instrumental music (fees vary), athletics, Portuguese after-school language program, chess club, and academic decathlon. **Average nightly homework:** 60 minutes, but varies by grade level. **Grading system for lower school:** O ("Outstanding"), S ("Satisfactory") and N ("Needs to Improve"). **Grading system for middle school:** Standard letter grades. **Frequency of parent/teacher conferences:** N/P. The school communicates with parents through conferences, progress reports, and voice mail. **Standardized test scores:** Provided to parents (own child's performance). **High schools attended by recent graduates:** "We feed into a number of Catholic high schools, including Bellarmine." **Other indicators that the school is accomplishing its goals:** "Our students are accepted to prestigious high schools."

ATHLETICS

Physical education program: N/P. **Interscholastic athletics:** The school provides "a number of after-school sports throughout the year." 5th-8th graders participate in the East Valley League.

Faculty

Gender: 60% female, 40% male. **Ethnicity:** 70% Caucasian (non-Latino), 30% Latino. **Highest educational degree held:** 80% Master's, 20% Bachelor's. **Credentials:** "Yes." **Teacher/student ratio:** 1:17 in lower school, 1:25 in middle school. **Faculty training and professional development:** The school requires all teachers to hold California teaching credentials. Teachers participate in in-service programs and continuing education.

Extended Care/After-School Programs

Extended care is provided mornings from 6 a.m. and afternoons until 6 p.m. **Cost:** $3/hour. **Drop-in:** Available. **No coverage on:** Holidays and vacations. **Snacks:** Provided. **Homework:** Program includes a homework center. **Staff/child ratio:** 1:7. **After-school classes:** The school also provides some free after-school activities.

Campus Life

Facilities: N/P. The campus includes a library. **Meals:** Lunch/meal service provided twice a week. **Transportation:** N/P. **Uniforms:** Yes. **Student support services:** N/P. **Services for children with learning differences:** One-on-one tutoring. **Counselor/student ratio:** "Varies." **Policies regarding discipline, drug/alcohol use and abuse prevention and AIDS awareness:** Zero tolerance. **Summer programs:** Summer school (currently $400 per session).

Parent Participation

Thirty-five volunteer service hours are required. **Fundraising:** Programs include scrip, jog-a-thon, candy fundraiser. **Parent education:** N/P.

What Sets the School Apart From Others?

"Five Wounds is culturally diversified and centered in academic excellence and spiritual formation."

THE GIRLS' MIDDLE SCHOOL

180 North Rengstorff Avenue
Mountain View, CA 94043
(650) 968-8338 *fax (650) 968-4775*
www.girlsms.org
gms@girlsms.org

Kathleen Bennett, *Founder and Head of School*
Holly Varian Zuklie, *Director of Admissions*

We are looking for "students who demonstrate an interest in school and developing a love of learning, who would thrive in a smaller, nurturing, all-girls' environment and whose parents understand and embrace our school vision. We rely on teacher recommendations, an interview, and prior assessment history as well as testing to determine if it is a good match between school and student." **Our school best serves** "bright, creative students who love school and want to be part of a small, challenging and fun school community."

GENERAL

Girls' day middle school. **Nonsectarian**. Founded 1998. **Nonprofit**. **Accreditation**: Candidate for WASC accreditation. **Enrollment**: 120 (G6-8). **Average class size:** 20. **Length of school year:** Approximately 172 days. **Length of school day:** 8:20 a.m.-3:15 p.m. **Location:** Between Central Expressway and Middlefield Road, next to a residential area.

STUDENT BODY

Geographic: Students come from Palo Alto, Menlo Park, Sunnyvale, East Palo Alto, Redwood City, San Jose, Mountain View and Los Altos. **Ethnicity:** 62% Caucasian, 16% Latina, 12% African-American, 9% Asian-American, 4% East Indian, 10% other. **Foreign students:** None. **Two f/t working parent families:** 85%. **Single parent families:** 8%.

ADMISSION

Application deadline: January 19 (call for exact date). **Application fee:** $60. **Application process:** Applicants must take the ISEE entrance exam, submit an application and participate in a family interview. All applicants are encouraged to arrange a shadow visit. **Admission test:** ISEE. **Test score/GPA cut-off:** N/P. **Number of applications received:** 120 applications were received last year for 40 spaces in 6th grade. Approximately five spaces in the 7th grade were open last year. **Preferences:** None defined.

Costs

Latest tuition: $12,500. **Last tuition increase:** Approximately 15%. **Tuition payment plan:** N/P. **Sibling discount:** N/P. **Percentage of students receiving financial aid:** Approximately 30%. **Average grant award:** $7,600. **Number full tuition grants:** None. **Number of partial tuition grants:** N/P. 88% of grants were half-tuition or more. **Other information regarding financial assistance:** All financial assistance is need-based.

Program and Philosophy

School's mission statement/goals. "The goal of the Girls' Middle School is to provide a place where girls from diverse backgrounds develop the academic skills, self-knowledge, and personal strength to achieve their dreams, as well as the empathy and communication skills to support each other on their journeys toward womanhood." **Academic program.** "The Girls' Middle School provides an academically challenging curriculum that encourages skill building, creativity, problem solving and critical thinking. Teachers strive to create an adventurous academic program, where girls learn that math, science, engineering and technology are fun and interesting. GMS emphasizes developing good study habits, follow-through, and personal responsibility in the academic realm." **Approach to teaching reading/math:** N/P (middle school). **Approach to technology and computer training:** Computer science is taught all three years of middle school by the computer science teacher. The school is dual-platform, with a Mac lab in one classroom and a PC lab in the other. In its first year, the school had a 2:1 student to computer ratio. The girls have access to the computers both during class time as well as during recess and lunch. All equipment is networked to a central server and has satellite access to the Internet. Computer programming is introduced into the curriculum in 7th grade. **Other courses/offerings:** Spanish, one-week camping trip at the beginning of the year, movement class 90 minutes/week which includes yoga, self-defense, modern dance, etc., engineering class to introduce students to structural and electrical engineering in 6th grade, and social and emotional learning classes to address issues of adolescent development and peer relationships. **Average nightly homework:** One hour in 6th grade with gradual increase in 7th and 8th grades. **Grading system:** No letter grades. Assessment is based on parent conferences, rubrics, progress reports and end-of-the-year narratives. **Frequency of parent/teacher conferences:** One scheduled parent conference per year, additional conferences are scheduled if necessary. Periodic written evaluations and progress reports are mailed home. An end-of-the-year narrative is also given to parents. **Standardized test scores:** Scores are provided to parents and school community (overall school performance). **High schools attended by recent graduates:** N/P. **Other indicators that the school is accomplishing its goals:** N/P.

ATHLETICS

Physical education programs: Four periods of physical education per week—two of "traditional" sports (outdoor sports and games) and a double block of movement class (see above). **Interscholastic athletics:** Basketball, soccer.

FACULTY

Gender: 20 teachers, all female. **Ethnicity:** 76% Caucasian, 8% Latina, 8% East Indian, 8% African-American. **Highest educational degree:** 50% Bachelor's, 36% Master's, 14% Doctorate. **Credentials:** 14% hold California teaching credential; 7% hold some other credential/training. **Teacher/student ratio:** 1:6 (average class size is 20). **Faculty selection and professional development:** Faculty are selected through "a rigorous and thorough screening process to find experienced and committed teachers." In-service training includes three in-service days during the school year and a summer-long curriculum workshop.

EXTENDED CARE/AFTER-SCHOOL PROGRAMS

N/P.

CAMPUS LIFE

Facilities: Currently housed in a leased school building space on church property in Mountain View. The library includes approximately 2,000 volumes. **Meals:** Optional hot lunch twice/week. **Transportation:** Limited van transportation is available, as well as a van shuttle to the CalTrain station. **Uniforms:** GMS shirt and any pants. **Co-curricular activities/clubs:** Science club, newspaper. **Student support services:** Counselor. **Services for children with learning differences:** No specialist on staff. **Counselor/student ratio:** 1:120. **Policies regarding discipline, drug/alcohol use and abuse prevention and AIDS awareness:** Zero tolerance policy for drugs on campus. Year-long class on social/emotional learning, which includes health issues and sex education. **Summer programs:** None.

PARENT PARTICIPATION

No minimum hours are required, but all parents volunteer. A parent association was recently established. **Parent education:** Monthly parent education evening. **Fundraising:** 100% participation in annual fund in first year.

WHAT SETS SCHOOL APART FROM OTHERS?

"Emphasis on empowering girls. Dynamic and challenging project-based math and science program which includes engineering and computer programming. Alternative assessment strategies without traditional grades and report cards. Fun, nurturing, inclusive, diverse learning environment."

How Do Parents/Students Characterize the School?

"It's fun, energized, creative, nurturing, challenging and empowering."

THE HARKER SCHOOL

500 Saratoga Avenue
San Jose, CA 95136
(408) 249-2510 *fax (408) 984-2325*

4300 Bucknall Road
Campbell, CA 95130
(408) 871-4600
www.harker.pvt.k12.ca.us

(From 2000-2001, Saratoga will house grades 6-11 and Bucknall K-5. Starting with the 2001-2002 school year, Saratoga will house 7-12 and Bucknall K-6.)

Howard Nichols, *President*
Diana Nichols, *Head of School*
Nan Nielsen, *Director of Admissions*

We are looking for "students who demonstrate the potential ability to be successful in a strong academic program." **Our school best serves** "students of average to above average ability with some academic background from their preschools, who are comfortable interacting with peers and adults."

General

Co-ed K-12 day and boarding school. Nonsectarian. Nonprofit. Accreditation: CAIS/WASC. Formed by the merger of the Palo Alto Academy (originally a college preparatory school for boys, founded in 1893) and the Harker Day School (a college preparatory school for girls, also originally in Palo Alto) in 1972. **Enrollment**: 1,035 in JuniorK-G8. **Average class size**: 16. **Length of school year**: Approximately 175 days. **Length of school day**: 8 a.m.- 3:30 p.m. **Location:** Due to the recent opening of its high school program, the school operates two campuses. The Saratoga campus is in northern San Jose, adjacent to Highway 280. The Bucknall campus is 2.8 miles away.

STUDENT BODY

Geographic: Most students come from communities in the Santa Clara County area, including Cupertino, Campbell, Los Altos, Palo Alto, Los Gatos, Milpitas, San Jose, Santa Clara, Saratoga, Sunnyvale, and Fremont. **Ethnicity:** 45% Caucasian, 30% Asian, 19% Middle Eastern or East Indian, 2% Latino, 2% African-American. **Foreign students (I-20 status):** 40. **Boarding students:** 60 (grades 5-8). **Two f/t working parent families:** 83%. **Single parent families:** 1%.

ADMISSION

Kindergarten. **Application deadline:** Early February. **Age requirement:** 5 years old by December 1. **Application fee:** $125. **Application process:** K and grade 1 includes individually administered IQ test and a classroom evaluation. **Preschools visited by admission director:** None. **Number of applications received:** 153 applications received last year for 59 spaces. 16 of 75 total K spaces taken by Jr. K students (school is phasing out Jr. K program). **Preferences:** Siblings, if equally qualified; staff children. **Other grades**. **Application deadline:** Early February. **Application fee:** $125. **Application process:** 1st grade, same as K. Grades 2 through 8, ERB CPT III (reading comp and math), teacher evaluation and report cards. **Test score/GPA cut-off:** 70th percentile (national norms). **Estimated number of openings in grades 1-8:** Approximately 5-10 per grade, depending on re-enrollment.

COSTS

Latest tuition: $13,200 (K-3rd grade), $14,200 (4th-6th grade), $15,200 (7th and 8th grade). **Last tuition increase:** Varies with each grade level. **Tuition payment plan:** Available through outside sources. **Sibling discount:** None. **Percentage of students receiving financial aid:** Approximately 10%. **Average grant award:** $8,130. **Number of full/partial tuition grants:** All tuition grants are partial tuition, 63% are half-tuition or more.

PROGRAM AND PHILOSOPHY

School's mission statement/goals: "The Harker School Philosophy: The Harker School, a co-educational, nonsectarian, college preparatory boarding and day school serving grades kindergarten through twelfth, strives to develop well-rounded citizens and life-long learners. Through comprehensive programs of sound academics and character development, the school provides a challenging and balanced education for college-bound students. [Mission Statement:] Academic excellence is achieved through the development of intellectual curiosity, personal accountability and a love of learning. Our comprehensive program and dedicated staff help students discover, develop and enjoy their unique talents. Kindness, respect and integrity are instilled within a safe and nurturing environment. We are a dynamic community that honors individuality, embraces diversity and prepares students to take their place as global citizens." **Academic program.** "The academic program is founded on the knowledge that students will respond to educators' expectations of them and strive to achieve the standards set for them. We set strong academic standards for all students. Language arts and math are offered at three levels: Grade level, grade level plus, and honors, allowing a student to be challenged to reach his best level without being stressed. Science (taught 5 days a week at all grade levels), P.E., art, music, drama and computer science classes are all taught by specialists in grades 1-8. Social studies and foreign language (Spanish grades 1-5, Spanish, French and Japanese in grades 6-8) are also integral parts of the curriculum. Students in grades K-3 are grouped by heterogeneous homerooms, except during language arts and math when they are grouped by their skill levels. Grades 4-8 are departmentalized." **Approach to teaching reading:** Phonics, patterns, and a literature-based series are integrated. **Approach to teaching math:** Computational skills are taught using manipulatives and are developed through practice and problem solving. Students are encouraged to explore alternative approaches to solving problems. At the early levels where reading levels might preclude a strong emphasis on problem solving, teachers include daily problems presented orally. **Approach to technology and computer training:** The school has four computer labs with 22 computers in each lab and four full-time instructors dedicated to computer training. All students receive computer instruction beginning in K. Age-appropriate curriculum includes keyboarding (beginning in 2nd grade), word processing, spreadsheets, Internet access and etiquette, e-mail, multimedia projects and an introduction to programming and computer-aided drawing in 7th and 8th grade elective courses. Computers are networked. Computer labs are available after school. The library has 15 computers available for use before and after school and at lunch. **Other courses/offerings:** Spanish (grades 1-8), French and Japanese (grades 6-8), art (K-8), music (choral, K-8), music (instrumental, piano, for additional fee), athletics (K-8), after-school sports (grades 4-8), dance (K-8), public speaking (grade 6), and drama (K-8). **Special programs:** Drama is part of the curriculum with grade level performances each year. 7th and 8th graders participate in a spring musical. Dance is available through P.E. and after school. The spring dance recital typically includes about 250 students each year. All grade levels participate in day field trips to local areas. Overnight trips include Coloma for 4th grade, Marin Headlands for 5th grade, Yosemite for 6th grade, Space Camp for 7th grade and Washington, D.C. for 8th grade. **Average nightly homework:** Beginning in 2nd grade, approximately 30 minutes per night, increasing to 2.5 hours by 8th grade. **Grading system:** Letter grades (A-F). **Frequency of parent/teacher conferences:** Held in fall. Report cards are issued four times per year. Teachers also communicate with parents on an as-needed basis by phone and e-mail. All teachers maintain their assignments on their web sites. **Standardized test scores:** Provided to parents; school performance provided to school community and parents of prospective students. **High schools attended by recent graduates:** The school recently added a high school. Prior to the addition of the high school, graduates attended Menlo, Castilleja, St. Francis, Mitty and Bellarmine, as well as eastern boarding schools such as Exeter, Choate and Deerfield. **Other indicators that the school is accomplishing its goals:** "Median child consistently scores above the independent median in all areas of the ERB."

ATHLETICS

Physical education program: Taught daily by specialists. The P.E. program emphasizes physical fitness as well as sports skill. Family life, health issues and drug education are included in the P.E. program. Both the lower and middle school campuses have a gymnasium and a swimming pool. **Interscholastic athletics:** Grades 4-8 participate in competitive sports such as volleyball, flag football, basketball, tennis, soccer, softball and track and field. The program has a "no-cut" policy: all students who wish to play are included on the team.

FACULTY

Gender: 69% female, 31% male. **Ethnicity:** 87% Caucasian, 5% Asian, 4% African-American, 2% Middle Eastern or East Indian, 2% Latino. **Highest educational degree earned:** N/P. **Teacher/student ratio:** 1:11 in lower school, 1:10 in upper school. **Faculty training and professional development:** Faculty selection is done through a screening program which includes interviews and an on-site demonstration teaching lesson.

EXTENDED CARE/AFTER-SCHOOL PROGRAMS

Before- and after-school supervision is provided from 7 a.m. to 6 p.m. for K-8. **Cost:** Included in tuition. **Drop-in:** Yes. **No coverage on:** School holidays. **Snacks:** None provided. **Homework:** Homework time for the majority of students is voluntary; a program that requires homework for students having difficulty is available. **Staff/student ratio:** N/P. **After-school classes:** Art, dance, drama, computers, cartooning, math, zoology, karate, etiquette, music appreciation, science club, safe child, playground, crafts, and study areas.

CAMPUS LIFE

Facilities: The school's K-4 campus consists of ten acres with three classroom buildings (a fourth is under construction), a multi-purpose room, gymnasium, locker rooms, basketball courts and a swimming pool. Grades five through high school are on a 16-acre campus with five academic buildings, dorm, gym, locker rooms, tennis courts, basketball courts and a swimming pool. Each campus has a library, 12,000 volumes total, with computers, electronic card catalogues, a research database containing over 5,000 periodicals, encyclopedias and Internet access. **Meals:** Hot lunch is available at an additional cost. **Transportation:** No school-sponsored transportation. The school assists with carpool information. **Uniforms:** Grades K-8. **Co-curricular activities/clubs:** Student government, after-school activities (see previous section). **Student support services:** Two full-time counselors do academic tracking and follow-up, also support with social and emotional issues. **Support for children with learning differences:** Teaching methods are adjusted to accommodate learning style differences. Tutoring referrals as needed. "We are not a school for children with severe learning differences." **Counselor/student ratio:** One counselor for grades K-4, one for grades 5 and 6, one for grades 7-8. **Policies regarding discipline, drug/alcohol use and abuse prevention and AIDS awareness:** "The school has a clearly identified discipline structure which focuses on allowing the teacher to spend time in the classroom teaching. Rules are defined and consequences are clearly stated. An initial warning is always given, followed by age appropriate detention and progressing to suspension for severe or repeated infractions. Phone calls to parents are an integral part of the process. The school has a no tolerance policy for drug and alcohol use, and drug and sex education are included in the P.E. program." **Summer programs:** Both a 3-week and 5-week summer session are offered, including academic mornings and day-camp activities in the afternoon. Costs range from $750 for a 3-week session, morning only, to $3,420 for 8-week full-day program.

Parent Participation

Participation is optional. Parents volunteer with classroom parties, field trips and other activities such as the annual fundraiser, and a family picnic. **Parent education:** The counseling department offers parenting classes. **Fundraising:** The major fundraiser is the family picnic. The school also conducts an annual giving campaign and capital campaigns for major building projects. Contributions are up to each family.

What Sets School Apart From Others?

"In a caring and supportive environment of small class sizes, faculty set strong expectations for academic achievement and courteous behavior. In class and out, faculty and staff help students develop personal responsibility for achieving academic success and a positive self-image. Science is a daily part of the curriculum and technology is integrated throughout. For Harker students, clubs, sports and activities ensure that school, and life, are more than just books."

How Do Parents/Students Characterize the School?

Parent response(s): Harker "provides a safe, academically challenging [environment] where each student's unique abilities are appreciated."

"The academics at Harker are superb, but what our family likes best is the character-building philosophy which permeates the entire Harker experience." "Our daughter is getting a superb education, and she's happy and eager to go to school—every morning of the week!"

THE HILLDALE SCHOOL

79 Florence Street (at Thiers)
Daly City, CA 94014
(650) 756-4737 *fax (650) 756-3162*

Tammy J. Long, *Head of School*

GENERAL

Co-ed K-5 school. **Nonsectarian**. Founded in 1962. Proprietary. **Accreditation**: "The Hilldale School has been in operation for 38 years." **Enrollment**: 150. **Average class size**: 15. **Length of school year**: 180 days. **School day:** 9 a.m. to 3:30 p.m. **Location:** In a residential neighborhood on San Bruno Mountain in Daly City, approximately 1.5 miles from the Daly City BART station.

STUDENT BODY

Geographic: Most students come from the upper Peninsula (San Bruno, Pacifica) and San Francisco. **Ethnicity:** The school's highest percentage is Asian students, followed by Latino, Caucasian, and African-American (percentages N/P). **Foreign students (I-20) status):** 0. **Two f/t working parent families:** 75%. **Single parent families:** 20%.

ADMISSION

<u>Kindergarten</u>. **Application deadline:** March 1. **Age requirement:** 5 years old by September. **Application fee:** $10. **Application process:** Tours are given Tuesday through Thursday mornings for 30 minutes. The extended care program is visited on the tours. An academic readiness test is administered to all applicants to the K program. K applicants are evaluated for "developmental readiness, including knowledge of numbers and letters, and of the world around them." **Preschools visited:** N/P. **No. of applications:** 40 applications were received for 28 places in latest K class. **Preferences:** Siblings. <u>Other grades</u>. **Application deadline:** Applications are accepted year-round. **Test score/GPA cutoff:** N/P. **Our school best serves**: N/P.

Costs

Latest tuition: $5,506, payable in 1, 2, 9, 10, or 12 installments. A 10% discount is allowed for full payment in advance. **Latest tuition increase:** 6%. **Tuition payment plan:** 10 monthly payments. **Sibling discount:** 10%. **Uniforms:** Required. **Other costs:** Approximately $90 for books and supplies, $32 for insurance and earthquake kit. **Financial aid:** None.

Academic Program

School's mission statement. "To provide a success-oriented program within a diverse student population, a program which nurtures and challenges the intellectual, emotional, physical, and social growth of each student while instilling the values of strong academic performance, self-discipline and a positive self-image." **Academic program.** "Hilldale School offers a rigorous academic program with small classes affording support for students of varying skill levels." **Approach to teaching reading:** "Reading is taught through a rigorous and systematic phonics program which enables students to quickly and effectively master the basic reading skills. In the later grades, the focus shifts to comprehension skills." **Approach to teaching math:** "Mathematics is taught in a similar manner with a progression from concrete to abstract experience in a sequential manner." **Approach to technology and computer training:** "Computer science is introduced at the kindergarten level and includes use of CD-ROMs and access to the Internet. Computers are in the classrooms, with Internet access." 2-4 computer for every 10-12 students. **Other courses/offerings** Spanish beginning in K. **Average nightly homework:** K-2 30 min. once a week, G3-5 45-60 min. 3-4 times a week. **Grading system:** Letter grades beginning in G4. **Frequency of parent teacher conferences:** Held twice a year between 3:30 p.m. and 8 p.m. **Standardized test scores:** N/P. **Middle schools attended by recent graduates:** Most graduating 5th graders attend the Discovery Center School, the sister school of the Hilldale School. **Other indicators that the school is accomplishing its goals:** N/P.

Athletics

Physical education program: Regular P.E. with instructor on staff. **Interscholastic athletics:** None, though many students participate in the Daly City Parks & Rec. program.

Faculty

Gender: 90% female, 10% male. **Ethnicity:** 90% Caucasian; 10% other. **Highest educational degree earned:** 30% have graduates degrees. **Teacher/student ratio:** 1:15. **Faculty training and professional development:** Average 15 hours continuing education training per year.

EXTENDED CARE PROGRAM

Morning care from 7 a.m. After-school care to 6 p.m. available to students in all grades, 80% of whom use it. Students in the extended care program play at indoor activities such as art, science, and computers in two large classrooms, or engage in outdoor sports and play in the school's large fenced playground. In the fall and spring, students also swim in the school's outdoor pool. **Cost:** No charge. Late pick-up fine of $10 per 15 minutes or fraction thereof. **Drop-in care:** Available at no charge. **Homework:** A supervised homework room is available daily from 3:30 p.m. to 4:30 p.m. for children doing homework. **Staff/student ratio:** Approximately 1 to 15. **Snacks:** Parents provide their child's snack. **After-school classes:** Each quarter different classes are offered. They have included cooking, video animation, science inventor's workshop, music, magic, outdoor sports, and calligraphy. **Cost:** Approximately $50-65 per session (approximately $6 per 50-60 min. class).

CAMPUS LIFE

Facilities: Four-acre campus including two converted residences, one with an outdoor in-ground pool, and outdoor play yards abutting a grove of Eucalyptus trees on San Bruno Mountain. A separate building houses the Kindergarten and after-school program. The school will be redesigning its play areas in the next few years. Small library. (N/P re print volumes, computers.) **Meals:** Students may buy lunches daily for $3.25. Parents receive each month's menu in advance and choose which days they want their child to order lunch. **Transportation:** None. **Uniforms:** Yes. **Co-curricular activities/clubs:** Student council, after-school clubs (classes). **Student support services:** N/P. **Support for children with learning differences:** "We recommend that parents avail themselves of the programs offered by their public school district. Teachers attend all IEP meetings." **Counselor/student ratio:** 0. **Policies regarding discipline, drug/alcohol use and abuse prevention and AIDS awareness:** N/P. **Summer programs:** The Hilldale School offers a summer program from approximately mid-June to the third week of August. Children swim daily in the school's outdoor pool. Swimming lessons (five Red Cross levels) and academic tutoring are offered. Extended care from 7 a.m to 6 p.m. is included in the cost. **Cost:** $135/week. Swimming lessons cost $25/week; recreational swimming, $15/week. Tutoring costs $45/week. The only days without coverage are five days between the end of the summer program and the beginning of the school year.

PARENT PARTICIPATION

Welcomed but not required. **Parent education:** N/P. **Fundraising:** None.

WHAT SETS SCHOOL APART FROM OTHERS

"Founded in 1962, The Hilldale School is a coeducational day school with an emphasis on traditional curriculum and high academic standards. Small classes provide maximum opportunity for learning for average and above average students. Located in a grove of Eucalyptus trees on a hilltop at the edge of San Bruno State Park, The Hilldale School offers a quality academic program in a country setting. Its small size and low teacher to student ratio afford each student individual attention. ... An enthusiastic staff and happy, motivated students make Hilldale a great place to learn."

HOLY FAMILY EDUCATION CENTER

4850 Pearl Avenue
San Jose, CA 95136
(408) 978-1355 *fax (408) 978-0290*
holyfamsj@aol.com

Gail Harrell, *Principal*

GENERAL

Co-ed K-8 Catholic parochial school (95% of students are Catholic). Founded in 1986. **Nonprofit. Accreditation:** WASC. **Enrollment:** 655. **Average class size:** 35. **Length of school year:** Approximately 180 days. **Length of school day:** 8 a.m.-2:45 p.m. **Location:** In a residential area of southwest San Jose. Accessible via Highway 85, Almaden Expressway exit.

STUDENT BODY

Geographic: Most students come from San Jose. **Ethnicity:** 61% Caucasian (non-Latino), 20% Latino, 7% Filipino, 7% Asian/Pacific Islander, 4% Middle Eastern or East Indian, 1% African-American. **Foreign students (I-20 status):** None. **Two f/t working parent families:** 60%. **Single parent families:** 15%.

ADMISSION

Kindergarten. Application deadline: February 15. **Age requirement:** 5 years old by December 1. **Application fee:** $35. **Application process:** After application is submitted, a screening date and time are set. Following the screening, a teacher evaluates with the principal. Students are prioritized and sent either acceptance, wait list or rejection letters. **Preschools visited by admission director:**

None. (The school operates its own PreK program.) **Number of applications received:** Approximately 75 applications received last year for 60 spaces, 38 of which were filled by students from the PreK program. **Preferences:** Siblings. **Other grades.** Same application deadline, fee and screening process. **Admission test:** Required. **Test score/GPA cut-off:** N/P. **Estimated number of openings in grades other than K each year:** 10 for grade 1, others vary. **"We are looking for ..."** N/P. **"Our school best serves ..."** N/P.

COSTS

Latest tuition: For K, $3,270 for in-parish, $3,550-$3,810 for out (depending on participation), and $4,200 for non-Catholic; for G1-8, $3,670 for in-parish, $4,000-$4,300 for out-of-parish, and $4,590 for non-Catholic. **Last tuition increase:** N/P. **Tuition payment plan:** Tuition is payable in annual, semi-annual, quarterly, monthly, or bi-monthly (direct debit) payments. **Sibling discount:** The total annual tuition for three or more children from a family that supports the parish is $9,080. The total for out-of-parish is $9,820, and $11,160 for non-Catholic. **Other:** Additional fees for after-school sports, 6th grade science camp, extended care, graduation, retreat (G7 and 8) and field trips. **Financial aid:** N/P.

PROGRAM AND PHILOSOPHY

School's mission statement. "The mission of Holy Family Educational Center is to foster and support the development of Catholic faith and identity while nurturing the whole child. In an academic environment, each child will grow in self-esteem, become cognizant of global issues and cultural diversity and participate in community service. We believe that this is a shared responsibility of the home, school and church." **Academic philosophy.** N/P. **Approach to teaching reading:** N/P. **Approach to teaching math:** N/P. **Approach to technology and computer training:** A new computer lab completed in 1999 has a dedicated instructor. It is available to grades 1-8. Computers are networked and allow Internet access. **Special programs:** Grade 8 play; grade 6 science camp; grade 7 retreat; grade 8 overnight retreat. **Other:** No foreign languages. "Art Vista" (arts program), music (choral). **Average nightly homework:** N/P. **Grading system for lower school:** "Outstanding," "Successful," "Improvement Needed." **Grading system for middle school:** Letter grades (A-F). **Frequency of parent/teacher conferences:** One mandatory conference per year; others upon request. **Standardized test scores:** Provided to parents (child's scores). **High schools attended by recent graduates:** 79% attended the six area Catholic schools, 21% attended public schools. **Other indicators that the school is accomplishing its goals:** N/P.

ATHLETICS

Physical education program: N/P. **Interscholastic athletics:** Grades 5-8 may participate in an inter-school athletic program.

FACULTY

Gender: 100% female. **Ethnicity:** 92% Caucasian (non-Latino), 4% other. **Highest educational degree held:** 80% Bachelor's, 20% Master's. **Credentials:** 96% California, 4% other. **Teacher/student ratio:** 1:35 (lower and middle school). **Faculty selection and professional development:** N/P.

EXTENDED CARE/AFTER-SCHOOL PROGRAMS

The program runs from 7 a.m.-6 p.m. for students in grades K-8. **Cost:** $25 annual family application fee, $2.50 per hour. **Drop-in:** Available. **No coverage on:** School holidays. **Snacks:** Provided. **Homework:** Assistance provided by staff. **Staff/student ratio:** N/P. **After-school classes:** Provided occasionally.

CAMPUS LIFE

Facilities: N/P. Campus includes library. **Meals:** N/P. **Transportation:** No school-sponsored transportation services. **Uniforms:** Uniforms and/or dress code. **Co-curricular activities/clubs:** N/P. **Student support services:** N/P. **Services for children with learning differences:** Learning lab. **Counselor/student ratio:** One counselor, two days per week. **Policies regarding discipline, drug/alcohol use and abuse prevention and AIDS awareness:** N/P. **Summer programs:** N/P.

PARENT PARTICIPATION

The school requires 40 hours for two-parent families, 20 hours for single-parent families. **Parent education:** Center for Family Development. **Fundraising:** N/P.

WHAT SETS SCHOOL APART FROM OTHERS?

N/P.

HOW DO PARENTS/STUDENTS CHARACTERIZE THE SCHOOL?

N/P.

KEYS SCHOOL

2890 Middlefield Road
Palo Alto, CA 94306
(650) 328-1711 *fax (650) 328-4506*
www.keysschool.com

Cheryl Rebischung, *Head of School*

We are looking for "social, emotional and academic readiness for our full-day program."

GENERAL

Co-ed K-8 day school. Nonsectarian. Founded 1973. **Nonprofit**, member CAIS, NAIS. **Accreditation:** CAIS. **Enrollment:** Approximately 175 (approximately 19 per grade). **Average class size:** N/P. **Length of school year:** N/P. **Length of school day:** 8:45 a.m.-3 p.m. (lower school), 8:30 a.m.-3:10 p.m. (middle school). **Location:** Central Palo Alto. Middlefield Road is accessible from Oregon Expressway, connecting to Highway 101 to the east and to Page Mill Road and Interstate 280 to the west.

STUDENT BODY

Geographic: A majority of students come from Palo Alto and neighboring communities of Menlo Park, Mountain View, and Los Altos. **Ethnicity:** 77% Caucasian (non-Latino), 12% Asian/Pacific Islander, 3% African-American, 4% Latino, 2% Middle Eastern or East Indian, 2% other. **Foreign students (I-20 status):** None. **Two f/t working parent families:** N/P. **Single parent families:** N/P.

ADMISSION

<u>Kindergarten</u>. **Application deadline:** January (call for date). **Application fee:** $50 (subject to change). **Application process:** Group screening (approximately 17 children at a time), teacher recommendation, and required parent interview. **Number of applications received:** 95 applications received for 20 spaces in K class last year. **Preferences:** Siblings. **Preschools visited by admissions director:** The admissions director visits several local preschools, including Bing, Montecito, Ta'Enna (JCC), and the Learning Center. **Other grades.** Student visit (full-day), teacher recommendation, records and testing results, parent interview. **Admissions test:** No separate formal testing. **Test score/GPA cut-off:** None. **Estimated number of openings in grades other than K each year:** 20 for all. **Other grades.** "We best serve students ..." N/P.

Costs

Latest tuition: $10,300 for K-4, $10,500 for 5-8 (including books, materials, field trips, etc.). **Latest tuition increase:** 11%. **Tuition payment plan:** "Available." **Sibling discount:** None. **Percentage of students receiving financial aid:** 6%. **Average grant award:** $6,360. **Number of partial tuition grants:** Eight, all of which were half tuition or more.

Program and Philosophy

School's mission statement/goals. "Keys School fosters the intellectual, physical and social growth of each student by providing a strong academic program in a caring and creative environment offering exceptional curricular diversity. ... Children learn basic skills, develop critical thinking and learn to express their ideas to others. Keys fosters intellectual, physical, social and emotional growth by providing a strong academic program enriched with the arts." **Academic program. Approach to teaching reading:** Students are provided specific instruction in phonics, vocabulary development, analytical and comprehension skills as well as in-depth exposure to trade books and selections from good literature. **Approach to teaching math:** The program is designed to "balance between computation and concepts, beginning with concrete number operations and culminating in the abstractions of algebra." **Approach to technology and computer training:** "In the computer lab, primary students learn basic file navigation as they explore software that integrates with reading, writing and math. By third grade, they learn basic keyboarding and word processing skills. Classroom computers allow students to follow up using software and skills taught during lab sessions." **Other courses/offerings:** Spanish readiness (K-3), Spanish instruction (grades 4-8), art (K-8), music, and Orff instruments. **Special programs:** Outdoor education program which includes program of ecological study at a nearby open-space preserve. Every grade also plans one or more trips to various environments throughout the state. "Drama is incorporated into the curriculum at every level, with each class presenting a production. 7th and 8th graders participate in an unique rotation that includes art, environment, drama and community service." **Average nightly homework:** Grades 1-8, 15 minutes to two hours. **Grading system for lower school:** Comments and checks. **Grading system for middle school:** Letter grades (A-F) and comments. **Frequency of parent/teacher conferences:** Held twice a year and as needed. **Standardized test scores:** Provided to parents only. **High schools attended by recent graduates:** Graduates go on to various Bay Area private high schools, including Crystal, Menlo, Woodside Priory, Castilleja and Sacred Heart Prep. **Other indicators that school is accomplishing its goals:** "Success of high school students, placements."

ATHLETICS

Physical education program: Emphasis on sportsmanship and team-sport skills (e.g., kick ball and ultimate ball). **Interscholastic athletics:** After-school sports program begins in 4th grade.

FACULTY

Gender: N/P. **Ethnicity:** N/P. **Highest educational degree earned:** N/P. **Credentials:** N/P. **Teacher/student ratio:** N/P. **Faculty training and professional development:** The school provides a "mentor program to provide support to new teachers, [and] strong teacher development."

EXTENDED CARE/AFTER-SCHOOL PROGRAMS

The school provides morning and afternoon programs. **Cost:** N/P. **Drop-in care:** Available. **No coverage on:** Holidays. **Snacks:** Provided to K only. **Homework:** Students are not required to complete homework in the after-school program. **Staff/student ratio:** N/P. **After-school activities/clubs/classes:** N/P.

CAMPUS LIFE

Facilities: The school's small campus includes a library, computer center and art room. The school uses Palo Alto city parks for sports fields. **Meals:** Lunch service provided. **Transportation:** School vans. **Uniforms:** None. "Simple" dress code. **Co-curricular activities/clubs:** N/P. **Student support services:** Include school counselor and learning specialist. **Services for children with learning differences:** N/P. **Counselor/student ratio:** N/P. **Policies regarding discipline/drug/ alcohol use and abuse prevention and AIDS awareness:** N/P. **Summer program:** Science Camp, Interim Program (each a 2-week program).

PARENT PARTICIPATION

N/P. **Parent education:** N/P. **Fundraising:** Parents are expected to participate in the annual giving program and help with the fundraising activities.

WHAT SETS SCHOOL APART FROM OTHERS?

"Happy environment, outstanding outdoor education. Rigorous yet balanced curriculum."

HOW DO PARENTS/STUDENTS CHARACTERIZE SCHOOL?

"Friendly, family-like."

LOS ALTOS CHRISTIAN SCHOOL

625 Magdelena Avenue
Los Altos, CA 94024
(650) 948-3738 *fax (650) 949-6092*
www.lacs.com

Sharon Sousa, *Principal* (ssousa@lacs.com)

We are looking for "students and families who value a Christ-centered education, Biblical teaching, academic challenge and a supportive school atmosphere."
Our school best serves "students who are developmentally ready to begin a formal reading, spelling, writing and math program at age five."

GENERAL

Co-ed PreK-6 Christian school (80% of student body are Christian). Preschool beginning age 3 through PreK. Founded in 1981. **Nonprofit. Accreditation:** WASC/ACSI. **Enrollment:** 233. **Average class size:** 25 in large and general education classes, 10 in small and special education classes. **Length of school year:** Approximately 180 days. **Length of school day:** 8:30 a.m.-3 p.m. **Location:** On Magdelena in a mostly residential area, between Foothill Expressway (to East) and Interstate 280 (to West).

STUDENT BODY

Geographic: Most students come from nearby communities of Los Altos, Mountain View, Cupertino, Sunnyvale, Palo Alto, Portola Valley, San Jose, and Menlo Park. **Ethnicity:** 75% Caucasian (non-Latino), 15% Asian/Pacific Islander, 5% Latino, 5% African-American. **Foreign students (I-20 status):** None. **Two f/t working parent families:** 50%. **Single parent families:** 50%.

ADMISSION

<u>Kindergarten</u>. **Application deadline:** The school begins accepting applicants from the host church, preschool and current families December 1. Applications are opened to the public January 1. **Age requirement:** 5 years old by September 1. **Application fee:** $50. **Application process:** Two teacher recommendations and work samples. Kindergarten applicants are given the Gesell Developmental Assessment to determine school readiness. All candidates and parents are interviewed by the administrator. Kindergarten teachers often observe candidates in a preschool setting, especially in the school's own preschool. **Preschools visited by admission director:** N/P. [Ed. Note: the school operates the Altos Oaks Preschool and Day Care Center on the same campus.] **Number of applications received:** 60 applications were received last year for 35 spaces. 10 spaces were filled by the school's preschool students. **Preferences:** Siblings, staff. <u>**Other grades.**</u> **Application deadline:** Applications are accepted on same schedule as described above for Kindergarten. **Application fee:** $50. **Application process:** Parents attend one of 10 scheduled observation days during the year prior to making the application, submit application and fee, and provide two confidential educational recommendations, work samples, and report cards. A full psycho-educational test battery including WISC III must be submitted for special education candidates. **Test score/GPA cut-off:** N/P. **Estimated number of openings in grades other than K each year:** Approximately 2 to 4 per grade level.

COSTS

Latest tuition: $3,780 in large class, $7,140 in small class. **Latest tuition increase:** Approximately 5%. **Tuition payment plan:** 10-month installment plan available. **Sibling discount:** Yes, though not applicable to "small class." **Percentage of students receiving financial aid:** Approx. 3%. **Average grant award:** $1,500. **Number of full tuition grants:** None. **Number of partial tuition grants:** 3-6. **Percentage that are half-tuition or more:** None. No financial assistance is available to students during their first year at LACS.

PROGRAM AND PHILOSOPHY

<u>School's mission statement/goals</u>. "To provide and maintain a regular course of study according to the standards of the California Department of Education, but with distinct instruction from a definitely Christian viewpoint as established by the Word of God in order that the students may grow in grace and in the knowledge of God through our Lord and Savior, Jesus Christ, and become worthy citizens of God's kingdom and our nation." **Academic program.** "There are five overarching institutional goals that guide the school—to integrate Christian truth into all aspects of daily life—to instill pure morals in the heart of the student—to generate a spirit of patriotism—to maintain high academic standards—to establish a pattern of self discipline in each student." **Approach to teaching reading:** The Slingerland approach is used in all classes in grades K-3; it is also used in

special education classes K-6 (teacher-directed approach with major phonics component plus higher thinking skills). **Approach to teaching math:** Saxon Math in K-6 (a teacher directed program teaching practical daily math use plus fundamental skills). **Approach to technology and computer training:** Technology committee oversees the design and implementation of technology within the school. The computer lab was completely renovated in August 1998 to include thirteen Gateway student computers and a destination monitor for group viewing of instructor's screen. The school has a full-time technology instructor, and keyboarding skills are taught in grades 3-6. Internet access is under the strict supervision of the instructor. In addition, each classroom has 1-3 computers per room. **Other courses/offerings:** French is offered after school (additional fee), art, choral music, after-school basketball (5th and 6th grades, for additional fee). **Special programs:** Off-site learning experiences (6-10 per year), on-site exhibits, assemblies or performing arts shows (2-6 per year). 4th grade overnight trip to "'49er Gold Rush Camp," 5th grade Outdoor Education Camp, 6th grade Discovery Voyage. **Average nightly homework:** 30-45 minutes (grades 1-3), 45-90 minutes (grades 4-6). **Grading system for K-1:** "Outstanding," "Satisfactory," "Needs Improvement." **Grading system for 2-6:** Letter grades (A-F). **Frequency of parent/teacher conferences:** Annual conferences and additional conferences on an "as-needed" basis. Teachers send home weekly notes and use e-mail and voice mail to communicate throughout the year. **Standardized test scores:** Provided to parents (individual scores), prospective parents and anyone who asks (school's overall performance). **Middle schools attended by recent graduates:** Southbay Christian, Kings Academy, Valley Christian Jr. High, Blach Middle School (public), Egan Middle School (public). **Other indicators that the school is accomplishing its goals:** "Comprehensive annual survey of parent opinion."

ATHLETICS

Physical education program: Focus on fitness, participation, effort, sportsmanship, skill. Two weekly sessions with P.E. instructor are required. The school has a gym. **Interscholastic athletics:** Private elementary school association. Basketball for grades 5 and 6 with separate boys' and girls' teams.

FACULTY

Gender: 95% female, 5% male. **Ethnicity:** 95% Caucasian (non-Latino), 5% Asian/Pacific Islander. **Highest educational degree held:** 95% Bachelor's, 5% Master's. **Credentials:** 95% hold California or out-of-state teaching credentials. 12 out of the 14 teachers have received Slingerland Teacher Training (the school sponsors the Slingerland Teacher Training course through Cal State Hayward in the summer). **Teacher/student ratio:** 1:25 in large classes, 1:10 in small classes. **Faculty selection and professional development:** Selection process includes observation at LACS, application, faculty committee and principal interview, and recommendation to board of directors. Teachers participate in 2-day educational conferences yearly and 1-3 individually selected workshops per teacher.

Extended Care/After-School Programs

Program is open mornings from 7:30 a.m. and afternoons until 6 p.m. Available to all grades. **Cost:** $150/month; $125 for after-school only. **Drop-in:** Available for $5/hour. **No coverage on:** School holidays. **Snacks:** Provided. **Homework:** 30 minutes of supervised study hall is required. **Staff/child ratio:** 1:12. **After-school classes:** Include French, drama and piano instruction (additional fees).

Campus Life

Facilities: The school is located on the seven-acre campus of the First Baptist Church of Los Altos, in three of the seven buildings on the site. A weekly chapel service is required of all students. The library is staffed with a full-time librarian and includes over 6,000 volumes, an automated catalog and check out system, and two Kurzweil Reading Systems for student use. **Meals:** Hot lunch available twice a week. **Transportation:** No school-sponsored transportation. **Uniforms:** Required. **Co-curricular activities/clubs:** Student council. **Student support services:** Learning Assistance Department for students with dyslexia, speech and language services, counseling services, resource program, on-site tutors, six Kurzweil Reading Systems for student use on the campus. **Services for children with learning differences:** See above. **Counselor/student ratio:** N/P. **Policies regarding discipline, drug/alcohol use and abuse prevention and AIDS awareness:** Signed behavioral standards on file for all students; discipline problems not handled by teachers are referred to the Dean of Students. Drug/alcohol usage or "talk" is grounds for dismissal. All lifestyle and family life education topics are presented in the context of Biblical standards. **Summer programs:** Two 4-week sessions. Slingerland summer school is required of new students entering the Learning Assistance Department. Fees available on request.

Parent Participation

Volunteers used "in every way we can." No minimum number of hours required. **Parent education:** Parent seminars six times per year for parents of dyslexic students. Parent Teacher Fellowship meets six times per year to discuss topics of interest to family life or education. **Fundraising:** The school sells scrip. No minimum purchase amount.

What Sets School Apart From Others?

"Staff provides strong Christian role models for children; effective teaching strategies used to develop spelling, reading and math proficiencies; unique program for students with dyslexia, which includes a variety of weekly opportunities to integrate into a General Education program; Extended Learning (Ex L) for students who particularly excel in creative writing and math."

How Do Parents/Students Characterize the School?

"Nurturing to students and families ... able to provide appropriate challenge for students with academic strengths as well as academic needs ... staff personnel are excellent, Godly role models for the children, children are seen as gifts for our families who have 'loaned them to us' for a season. ... The home and school stand in partnership—both having the best interest of the child in mind."

MENLO SCHOOL

50 Valparaiso Avenue
Atherton, CA 94027
(650) 330-2000 *fax (650) 330-2006*
www.menloschool.org

Norman Colb, *Head of School*
Jennifer Weber, *Director of Middle School Admissions*

We are looking for "students who love learning, who truly enjoy working cooperatively with others, who are well-rounded and have a passion for something that can enrich our community (i.e., art, music, athletics, community)." **Our school best serves** "students who love learning, are motivated to do their personal best, and have a desire to be part of a community of learners."

General

Co-ed day middle and high school. Nonsectarian. Founded 1915. **Nonprofit**, member of CAIS, NAIS. **Accreditation:** WASC. **Enrollment**: 220 in middle school, 520 in high school (approximately 88-90% of middle-school students move on to upper-school program). **Average class size:** 18. **Length of school year:** 179. **Length of school day:** 7:50 a.m.-3:30 p.m. ("includes athletic/sports practice time"). **Location:** Approximately one block west of El Camino Real, in Atherton, a small suburban community between Redwood City and Menlo Park.

Student Body

Geographic: Most students come from Palo Alto, Menlo Park, Atherton, Woodside, Portola Valley, San Mateo, and San Carlos. **Ethnicity:** 80% Caucasian (non-Latino), 10% Asian/Pacific Islander, 4% Filipino, 3% Latino, 3% African-American. **Foreign students (I-20 status):** None. **Two f/t working parent families:** 30%. **Single parent families:** 15%.

ADMISSION

Application deadline: January (check with school for date). **Application fee:** $50. **Application process:** Essays, teacher recommendations, principal recommendation, testing, visit, interview and transcripts. **Number of applications received:** 4 to 5 applications for each space last year. **Admission test:** N/P. **Test score/GPA cut-off:** N/P. **Preferences:** Sibling, alumni and faculty child preferences given "if the school is a good educational match for the applicant." **Estimated number of openings in grades other than 6th each year:** 1-2.

COSTS

Latest tuition: $15,625 (includes lunch). **Last tuition increase:** Approximately 7.8%. **Tuition payment plan:** A 10-month payment plan is available. **Sibling discount:** None. **Percentage of students receiving financial aid:** 15-18% (varies by year). **Average grant award:** $10,700. **Number of full tuition grants:** None. **Number of partial tuition grants:** 83; 60% of grants are half-tuition or more. **Other information regarding financial assistance:** "All financial aid awards are need-based. We do not award grants for academic, athletic or other merit. The financial process is confidential and separate from the admissions process. Families must fill out the PFS form and mail it to Princeton, New Jersey as well as provide a 1040 income tax return."

PROGRAM AND PHILOSOPHY

School's mission statement/goals. Statement of Mission and Purpose: "Menlo School is dedicated to providing a challenging academic curriculum complemented by outstanding fine arts and athletic programs. The school helps students to develop positive values and nurtures character development in a supportive environment which upholds the highest moral and ethical standards. Menlo's program encourages students to reach their fullest potential, developing the skills necessary to respond intelligently and humanely to the complexities of an increasingly diverse world." **Academic philosophy.** "Menlo provides middle school students with an engaging and rigorous academic experience in a nurturing and supportive community. To accomplish this goal Menlo offers small classes of 18, an integrated and interdisciplinary curriculum, and a broad range of athletics and extracurricular activities. At the heart of the program is an extraordinarily talented and dedicated group of teachers who are both passionate about learning and deeply committed to the success of every child in the school. Middle School students take a series of core classes, which include English, Social Studies/History, Math, and Science. Students also choose from one of four foreign languages (French, Japanese, Latin or Spanish). All students take a rotation of arts and enrichment classes, which includes art, computers, drama, human skills and music." **Special programs:** Two middle school drama productions each year. All students take fine arts as part of the curriculum, and can also participate in the jazz band, chorus or drama club. **Average nightly homework:** Two hours in 6th grade, 2.5 hours in 7th, 3 hours in 8th grade. **Grading system:** A-F with narratives plus additional marks for effort, participation and citizenship. **Frequency of parent/teacher conferences:** Two parent/teacher conferences each year. Teachers also communicate through progress reports, phone calls and quick notes. **Standardized test scores:** Provided to parents (child's test scores). **High schools attended by recent graduates:** N/P. (School is 6-12.) **Other indicators that the school is accomplishing its goals:** "Parent feedback in a variety of ways, student and faculty retention, student portfolio reviews, test scores, and the number of 8th graders who are promoted to 9th grade."

ATHLETICS

Physical education program: "All middle school students participate in either the P.E. program or athletics. The athletic program is built into the school day." **Interscholastic athletics:** "All students are eligible to play inter-scholastic athletics at the middle school level. Menlo is a member of the Parochial Athletic Conference. The school offers 13 sports and 38 teams."

FACULTY

Approximately 24 full-time and part-time teachers in the middle school. **Gender:** 66% female and 33% male. **Ethnicity:** N/P. **Highest educational degree held:** 80% Master's, 19% Bachelor's, 1% Doctorate. **Credentials:** N/P. **Teacher/ student ratio:** 1:8.5. **Faculty training and professional development:** Menlo conducts three in-services for faculty each year and also offers a summer grant program allowing faculty to apply for grants to study a topic unrelated to their subject area.

CAMPUS LIFE

Facilities: Menlo School is located on 64 oak-studded acres in Atherton. The school is adjacent to, but now operated separately from, Menlo College. The campus buildings range from a converted mansion to modest, semi-portable classrooms. The school recently completed construction of a new middle school campus, which includes five new buildings, 15 classrooms, a theater and library. The library, newly constructed in 1998, holds 15,000 volumes, 42 computers and a separate media room. **Meals:** Lunch is provided. The cost is included in tuition. **Transportation:** No school-sponsored transportation. **Uniforms:** None; casual dress code. **Co-curricular clubs activities/clubs:** Chorus, jazz band, chess, yearbook, book club, foreign language clubs, computers, historical films, drama, literary magazine, debate, math olympiad. **Student support services:** Students are assigned a faculty advocate. Small advocacy groups (12 students) meet twice a week for student support. **Services for children with learning differences:** Limited service. **Counselor/student ratio:** N/A. **Discipline, drug/alcohol abuse prevention/AIDS awareness:** "The School Handbook outlines the policies and disciplinary process for violation of the values and expectations of the school community." **Summer programs:** Summer Explorations Program ($800 for 3 weeks; $1,500 for 6 weeks).

PARENT PARTICIPATION

Organized through Menlo School Association (MSA), "a parent organization that provides a wide range of support, feedback, appreciation, volunteer time and development resources." Monthly meetings are held to provide an open forum for parents. **Parent education:** Menlo offers three grade-level parent education seminars each year on topics concerning the nature of middle school learners and a variety of developmental issues. **Fundraising:** Annual Fund, Annual Fundraiser benefit.

WHAT SETS SCHOOL APART FROM OTHERS?

"The middle school program at Menlo is designed around the specific needs of young learners. Middle school students also have a distinct part of campus to call their own. They have their own space to learn, play and grow. Most classes meet in ninety-five minute blocks and the curriculum is integrated and reinforced across subject areas. There is ample time for hands-on experiments and meaningful discussions. The teachers are organized in grade level teams around students, rather than around departments. Teachers have ninety-five minutes a day to plan curriculum and discuss student progress. Menlo also offers a wide range of clubs as well as a comprehensive middle school athletic program in which all students are able to participate at a wide range of skill levels."

MID-PENINSULA JEWISH COMMUNITY DAY SCHOOL

4000 Terman Drive
Palo Alto, CA 94306
(650) 494-8200 *fax (650) 424-0714*
www.mpjcds.org
janet_newman@mpjcds.org (elementary school)
eric_keitel@mpjcds.org (middle school)

Gary Elgarten, *Head of School*
Eric Keitel, *Head of Middle School*

We are looking for "a diverse group of students and families who exhibit enthusiasm for learning, a love of Judaism, and a wish to grow emotionally, spiritually and intellectually within a nurturing and supportive environment." **Our school best serves** "students who are passionate about learning, enjoy working cooperatively with other learners, and who are interested in being part of a loving community."

GENERAL

Co-ed K-8 Jewish community day school (100% of students are Jewish). Founded in 1989. **Nonprofit. Accreditation:** CAIS. **Enrollment:** 300 (split between 215 in elementary and 85 in middle school). **Average class size:** 24 (with 2 full-time teachers) in elementary grades, 18 in middle school. **Length of school year:** Approximately 175 days. **Length of school day:** 8:30 a.m. to 3:30

p.m. **Location:** Off of Arastradero Road, between Foothill Expressway and El Camino Real.

STUDENT BODY

Geographic: Most students come from Palo Alto, Los Altos and Mountain View. The school also has students from Atherton, Redwood City, San Carlos, San Mateo, Fremont, Sunnyvale, Los Gatos, San Jose and Menlo Park. **Ethnicity:** 86% Caucasian (non-Latino), 10% Middle Eastern or East Indian, 3% Asian or Pacific Islander, 1% African-American. **Foreign students:** None. **Boarding students:** None. **Two f/t working parent families:** 60%. **Single parent families:** 5%.

ADMISSION

Kindergarten: Application deadline: January 1. **Age requirement:** 5 years old by September 1. **Application fee:** $60. **Application process:** Preschool recommendation, school visit/screening, and parent interview screening. **Preschools visited by admission director:** Albert L. Schultz JCC Preschool and Bing Preschool. **Number of applications received:** 90 K applications for 48 spaces. **Preferences:** Siblings and children of faculty. **Other grades. Application deadline:** January 1. **Application fee:** $60. **Application process:** For 1st-5th grade and middle school, teacher recommendation, transcripts, school visit, parent interview and standardized test scores. Middle school applicants also undergo academic screening. **Test score/GPA cut-off:** None. **Estimated number of openings in grades other than K each year:** 1-2 (other than 6th). 60 applications were received last year for 36 spaces in 6th grade.

COSTS

Latest tuition: $8,550 for K-5, $9,550 for 6-8. **Latest tuition increase:** Approximately 8%. **Tuition payment plan:** 10-month payment plan available. **Sibling discount:** 10%. **Percentage of students receiving financial aid:** 15%. **Average grant award:** Approximately 35% of tuition. **Number of full tuition grants:** None. **Number of partial tuition grants:** 45. **Percentage that are half-tuition or more:** 50%.

PROGRAM AND PHILOSOPHY

School's mission statement/goals: "MPJCDS is dedicated to a rich, diverse and caring educational process. Our students develop personal values, including a love of learning, respect for others, pride in their Jewish heritage, and a deep commitment to tikkun olam (perfecting the world), the practice of tzedakah (acts of charity) and gemilut chassadim (compassion towards others)." **Academic philosophy:** "MPJCDS provides a excellent integrated academic program in both secular and Judaic studies. Our emphasis is on developing a lifelong capacity for independent critical thinking, self-motivated learning, and academic achievement.

We utilize a hands-on experiential approach that affords students the opportunity to utilize all of their intelligences." **Approach to teaching reading:** "A balance between phonics-based and literature-based instruction, guided reading, shared reading, small group instruction." **Approach to teaching math:** Grades K-5, Everyday Math (a University of Chicago program with an emphasis on problem solving and critical thinking). In grades 6-8, Connected Mathematics with advanced groups (includes algebra and geometry in 7th and 8th grades). **Other:** Hebrew instruction K-8th, Spanish as 8th grade elective, art, music (choral and instrumental - no additional fee), and athletics twice weekly. **Approach to technology and computer training:** Technology instruction is integrated into the curriculum. State of the art multi-media center in addition to computers in each classroom. Full internet access/network throughout school. The computer lab is open at lunch and after school. **Special programs:** For elementary school students, After School Players (drama), chess club, and 4th grade gold country trip. For middle school students, 6th grade science education trip to Yosemite, 7th grade Oregon Shakespeare and Los Angeles museum trips, 8th grade trip to Boston/Washington D.C. **Average nightly homework:** 15 minutes (K), 20-30 minutes (grades 1 and 2), 30-45 minutes (grades 3-5), 75-120 minutes (grades 6-8). **Grading system for lower school:** Written evaluations twice a year and portfolio assessment. **Grading system for middle school:** Narratives twice a year and letter grades twice a year. **Frequency of parent/teacher conferences:** Two parent conferences per year (student-led from grade 4 up). **Standardized test scores:** Provided to parents (child's scores), school community (school's overall performance), and prospective parents. **Middle schools attended by recent graduates:** The school now has its own middle school program with its first graduating class in June 2001. Previous graduates have attended middle school at Crystal Springs, Menlo, Nueva, Harker, Jordan (Palo Alto public school), and JLS (Palo Alto public school). **Other indicators that the school is accomplishing its goals:** "Excellent retention rate; very few students leave the school prior to graduating."

ATHLETICS

Physical education program: Twice weekly P.E. class focusing on team building and cooperation, coordination, and team sports. The school has use of an indoor gymnasium and an outdoor soccer field/play space. **Interscholastic athletics:** After-school parent-governed soccer leagues (competing with other independent schools).

FACULTY

Gender: 85% female, 15% male. **Ethnicity:** 80% Caucasian (non-Latino), 15% Middle Eastern or East Indian, 5% Latino. **Highest educational degree held:** 60% Master's, 35% Bachelor's, 5% Doctorate. **Credentials:** More than 90% hold California teaching credentials. Some teachers hold certification from other states or Israel (Hebrew teachers). **Teacher/student ratio:** 1:12 in lower school,

1:15 in middle school. **Faculty selection and professional development:** Faculty are selected through interviews with administration and faculty, model lessons, resumes, and references. Faculty training includes three full in-service days and a two-week summer planning session. Attendance at conferences is encouraged.

Extended Care/After-School Programs

After-school care from 3:30 to 5:45 p.m. **Cost:** $25 per day. **Drop-in:** Not available. **No coverage on:** School holidays. **Snacks:** Provided. **Homework:** Mandatory; full-time teacher supervises. **Staff/child ratio:** 1:10. **After-school classes:** After-School Players (drama), chess club. **Cost:** "Minimal."

Campus Life

Facilities: The school is located on a 1.5-acre campus adjacent to the Albert L. Schultz Jewish Community Center in Palo Alto. A new school building was constructed last year with 12 classrooms, library, and multi-media technology lab. Plans are underway to construct a multi-purpose room and gymnasium. **Meals:** Meal service is available daily. **Transportation:** Bus service from Los Gatos to Palo Alto (round trip). **Uniforms:** None; casual dress code. **Co-curricular activities/clubs:** In lower school, math olympiads and chess (offered as electives). In middle school, yearbook, cooking, creative writing, self-defense, orchestra, computer programming and drama. **Student support services:** Part-time resource specialist, part-time counselor. Middle school students are assigned a faculty advisor (1:10 ratio). Advisory groups meet weekly for facilitated discussions on ethics, values and student issues. **Services for children with learning differences:** Part-time resource specialist. **Counselor-student ratio:** 1:300. **Policies regarding discipline, drug/alcohol use and abuse prevention and AIDS awareness:** Upper elementary and middle school students receive instruction as part of their science curriculum. **Summer programs:** A one-week summer camp is offered in the latter part of June.

Parent Participation

Parents are asked to volunteer 25 hours per school year in support of the school's programming and fundraising. **Parent education:** Parent Kesher (parent organization) offers monthly opportunities for workshops and study. The school also communicates with parents through a weekly newsletter, and weekly parent coffee hours. **Fundraising:** Annual "Balance the Books" campaign, based on ability to give and annual Purim Ball.

What Sets School Apart From Others?

MPJCDS faculty and staff are formally trained in the Responsive Classroom model of social and emotional literacy. Using this methodology, along with the strong ethical teachings of modern Judaism, we are able to instill in our students a strong moral and ethical code of behavior. This enables our students to be fully available for the enriched and rigorous academic program we offer throughout the school. Our elementary school model of two full-time teachers in each classroom allows flexibility in grouping students most effectively. Our middle school faculty operate as a team, integrating curriculum and fostering thematic study. Our middle schoolers participate in a comprehensive service learning program which builds connections to community and awareness of the world outside the classroom."

How Do Parents/Students Characterize the School?

"Our school teaches us to go above and beyond."
"The school is like my second home."
"At school, we develop close ties and friendships. The other kids and teachers are like family to me."

MOST HOLY TRINITY SCHOOL

1940 Cunningham Avenue
San Jose, CA 95122
(408) 729-3431 *fax (408) 272-4945*
www.dsj.org/edu/most.htm

Connie McGhee, *Principal*
Mrs. Leatrice Toller, *Assistant Principal*

We are looking for "children and families who value strong academic, spiritual and social development of children and are willing to be our partners." **Our school best serves** "families who believe in living the Word of God and actively pursue academic excellence while fostering a high level of personal dignity."

General

Co-ed K-8 Catholic parochial school (99% of students are Catholic). Founded in 1965. **Nonprofit. Accreditation:** WASC (through June 2003). **Enrollment:** 297. **Average class size:** 35. **Length of school year:** 180 days. **Length of school day:** 8 a.m.-3 p.m. **Location:** East of Highway 101 and south of the Interstate 280/680 connector. Accessible via Highway 101, Story Road exit.

Student Body

Geographic: Most students come from the communities of San Jose, Sunnyvale, Milpitas, and Santa Clara. **Ethnicity:** 45% Latino, 36% Filipino, 13% Caucasian (non-Latino), 6% Asian/Pacific Islander, 1% African-American. **Foreign**

students (I-20 status): None. **Two f/t working parent families:** 87.5%. **Single parent families:** 1%.

Admission

Kindergarten. **Application deadline:** Begins February 1. **Age requirement:** 5 years old by December 1. **Application fee:** $25. **Application process:** Kindergarten teacher and/or designated teacher administers a kindergarten readiness test and ranks students as "good," "OK," or "low." **Preschools visited by admissions director:** None. **Number of applications received:** 65 applications received last year for 65 spaces. **Preferences:** Siblings, Catholics, active parishioners. **Other grades. Application deadline:** After February 1, until spaces are filled. **Application fee:** $25. **Application process:** Mastery curriculum tests in reading, mathematics, and writing at grade level, current standardized test results (e.g., Stanford Achievement). **Admission test:** Admission test given April-June. **Test score/GPA cut-off:** SAT at grade level or above; curriculum mastery at grade level or above. **Estimated number of openings in grades other than K each year:** 15.

Costs

Latest tuition: For K, $2,476 for in-parish, $3,095 for out, and $3,343 for non-Catholics; for G1-8, $2,814 for in-parish, $3,517 for out, and $3,799 for non-Catholics. **Last tuition increase:** Approximately 7.4%. **Tuition payment plan:** 10-month plan available, or 5% discount for payment in full. **Sibling discount:** Substantial. **Percentage of students receiving financial aid:** 10%. **Average grant award:** $1,000. **Number of full tuition grants:** 7, 3 of which are half tuition or more. **Other information regarding financial assistance:** "Special arrangements are made whenever unforeseen emergencies/circumstances emerge. The school currently enjoys the benefits of a benefactor endowment which helps provide tuition assistance, coupled with Catholic Diocese support."

Program and Philosophy

School's mission statement/goals. "Most Holy Trinity School is a culturally diverse Catholic community of students, staff and parents. Together, we are called upon to live the Word of God through reflection, celebration and action. Most Holy Trinity School, united with the programs of Most Holy Trinity Parish, other communities and agencies, is committed to empowering our students to live integrated, responsive, Christian life in the twenty-first century. We accomplish this through the development of spirituality, academic excellence, personal growth and outreach." **Academic philosophy.** "We as the Most Holy Trinity School community believe in living the Word of God and actively pursuing academic excellence, while fostering a high level of personal dignity. We assume collaborative responsibility for our students' positive growth and development. We strive to enhance the lives of those in our school community." **Academic program.**

Approach to teaching reading: "The faculty utilizes a variety of resources, activities and teaching styles while integrating content and skill in order to meet the individual needs of students. A literature rich environment." **Approach to teaching math:** "The faculty provides a systematic development of skills in mathematics. Students are encouraged to be mathematically powerful—that is to say they are expected to think, communicate and problem solve, drawing on mathematical ideas and using mathematical concepts." **Approach to technology and computer training:** "Follow Diocesan Technology Goals. Curriculum focuses on student. Expected outcomes at grade level; new i-Mac Lab available to all grade levels 50-80 minutes/week and technology available at all grade levels in classrooms." **Other courses/offerings:** ArtPath Artist-in-Residence collaborative with San Jose State University, music (choral), athletics. **Special programs:** After-school multi-cultural creative and performing arts program in collaboration with City of San Jose arts project; 6th grade outdoor school (4-day program); 8th grade spiritual retreat at Asilomar (3 days). **Average nightly homework:** 30 minutes (grades 1-3); 60-80 minutes (grades 4-6); 80-120 minutes (grades 7-8). **Grading system for grades 1-3:** "Satisfactory" and "Needs Improvement." **Grading system for grades 4-8:** Letter grades (A-F). **Frequency of parent/teacher conferences:** "Frequent sign-off on progress." One formal conference per year and as needed. **Standardized test scores:** Provided to parents (child's scores), school community (school's overall performance), parents of prospective students and anyone else who asks. **High schools attended by recent graduates:** Notre Dame (5), Mitty (4), Presentation (3), St. Lawrence (1), Liberty Baptist (1), Bellarmine (5), public schools (13). **Other indicators that the school is accomplishing its goals:** Student awards and recognition. Annual gains on national SAT scores.

ATHLETICS

Physical education program: "Participation in physical activity and sports is a necessary part of the development of a child as a whole person." Each student has two periods of P.E. per week. **Interscholastic athletics:** "The After-School Sports Program is for all interested students in Grades 5-8. The program includes flag football, volleyball, basketball, softball and track."

FACULTY

Gender: 80% female, 20% male. **Ethnicity:** 69% Caucasian (non-Latino), 23% Latino, 8% Filipino. **Highest educational degree held:** 67% Bachelor's, 27% Master's, 7% Doctorate. **Credentials:** 73% California. **Teacher/student ratio:** 1:35. **Faculty training and professional development:** Teachers hired must have teaching credential; 30 hours of in-service per year.

EXTENDED CARE/AFTER-SCHOOL PROGRAMS

Extended care is available from 7 a.m. until class begins and after school until 6 p.m. **Cost:** $3.75/hour. **Drop-in:** Available for $5/hour. **No coverage on:** Labor Day, Columbus Day, Thanksgiving, Christmas, New Year's Day, Martin Luther

King Jr. Day, Easter, Memorial Day, and President's Day. **Snacks:** Provided. **Homework:** Homework Club, a teacher-staffed, voluntary homework program. **Staff/child ratio:** 1:20. **After-school classes:** N/P.

CAMPUS LIFE

Facilities: Featured facility is the newly refitted i-Mac computer lab. The library and media center are newly computerized. **Meals:** Hot lunch is provided by a neighboring public school. **Transportation:** No school-sponsored transportation. **Uniforms:** School uniforms and P.E. uniforms are required. **Co-curricular activities/clubs:** Student council (grades 5-8), booster club (8th grade), academic decathlon (grades 7-8), toastmaster's (grades 7-8), and talent show (grades 4-8). **Student support services:** Homework club (grades 6-8), reading and math support if student's score is below 30% on SAT. **Services for children with learning differences:** Coordinate with public school for pullout services. **Counselor/student ratio:** 1/2 full-time equivalent. [Ed. note: Approximately 1:594.] The school provides "push-in" guidance lessons to all grade levels. **Policies regarding discipline, drug/alcohol use and abuse prevention and AIDS awareness:** "Diocesan required family life and substance abuse curriculum is provided." **Summer programs:** None.

PARENT PARTICIPATION

50 volunteer hours for 2-parent families, 25 hours for single-parent families. "Volunteers are encouraged and provide 1-1 assistance with field trip supervision, parish activities and extensive parent support activities." **Parent education:** Parent education sessions (4-5 per year, 1.5 hours) are provided in the evening. **Fundraising:** The school scrip program, which includes over 38 participating vendors; $3,500 per family per year required.

WHAT SETS SCHOOL APART FROM OTHERS?

"Our school is very peaceful and education and services are highly personalized. Our ethnic and linguistic diversity are strengths. Our parents are singularly involved and supportive. Our children are highly motivated and focused on service to our community and high academic achievement."

HOW DO PARENTS/STUDENTS CHARACTERIZE THE SCHOOL?

"The school has a feeling of 'family' to it that was apparent from the first year. We have a home-like atmosphere with a lot of warmth. Our students are supportive of each other, showing a Christian way of caring for one another."

NOTRE DAME ELEMENTARY SCHOOL

1500 Ralston Avenue
Belmont, CA 94002
(650) 591-2209 *fax (650) 591-4798*
www.belmont.gov/educ/ndes

Dolores Quigg, SND, *Principal*

GENERAL

Co-ed 1st-8th grade independent Catholic school, operated by the Sisters of
Notre Dame de Namur. (90% of students are Catholic.) Founded 1851. **Nonprofit. Accreditation:** WASC (through 2001). **Enrollment:** 260. **Average class
size:** 30-35. **Length of school year:** 180 days. **Length of school day:** 8:20 a.m.-
3 p.m. **Location:** Between Highways 101 and 280 in Belmont, a suburban community approximately 17 miles south of San Francisco.

STUDENT BODY

Geographic: Most students come from San Mateo County communities.
Ethnicity: 70% Caucasian (non-Latina), 10% Filipina, 10% Asian/Pacific Islander, 5% Middle Eastern or East Indian, 5% Latina. **Foreign students (I-20
status):** Less than 1% (one student). **Two f/t working parent families:** 80%.
Single parent families: 5%.

ADMISSION

<u>First grade</u>. **Application deadline:** March 10. **Age requirement:** 6 years old by
September 1. **Application fee:** $30. **Application process:** A visit to the school
and testing on a Saturday in March. **Preschools visited by admissions director:**
N/A. **Number of applications received:** N/P. **Preferences:** Siblings, children of
alumnae, faculty children. <u>Other grades</u>. **Application deadline:** March 10. **Application fee:** $30. **Application process:** A visit to the school and testing on a
Saturday in March. **Test score/GPA cut-off:** N/P. **Estimated number of openings in grades other than 1st each year:** N/P. **"We are looking for "** N/P. **"Our
school best serves ..."** N/P.

COSTS

Latest tuition: $3,300 + $440 registration and $155 books (= $3,895). **Latest
tuition increase:** N/P. **Tuition payment plan:** Available. **Sibling discount:** "Yes."
Financial aid: N/P.

PROGRAM AND PHILOSOPHY

School's mission statement/goals. N/P. **Academic program.** Curriculum includes Spanish instruction every day in grades 1-8, music (choral and recorders), and athletics. **Approach to teaching math/reading:** N/P. **Approach to technology and computer training:** Ratio of 1:5 computers to students, a full-time technical coordinator, networked, web page, "junior webmasters" program and "all teachers qualified on computers." **Special programs:** Outdoor education (6th grade), ropes program (7th grade), retreat (8th grade), and chorus. **Average nightly homework:** N/P. **Grading system:** N/P. **Frequency of parent/teacher conferences:** Two formal scheduled conferences and as needed. **High schools attended by recent graduates:** N/P. **Other indicators that the school is accomplishing its goals:** N/P.

ATHLETICS

Physical education program: N/P. **Interscholastic athletics:** Catholic School League for grades 4-8 in baseball, basketball, track and tennis.

FACULTY

Gender: 85% female, 15% male. **Ethnicity:** N/P. **Highest educational degree held:** N/P. **Credentials:** All have California teaching credentials. **Teacher/student ratio:** 1:15. **Faculty selection and professional development:** "A variety of in-service [and by] encouraging professional organization membership."

EXTENDED CARE/AFTER-SCHOOL PROGRAMS

N/P.

CAMPUS LIFE

Facilities: Notre Dame Elementary is one of four schools on a campus that is the site of the former Ralston-Sharon Estate (other schools are a preschool, Notre Dame High School and College of Notre Dame). The school has a library (N/P re volumes etc.). **Meals:** Available once/week. **Transportation:** No school-sponsored transportation. **Uniforms:** Yes. **Co-curricular activities/clubs:** Computers, science and sports. **Student support services:** Counselor. **Counselor/student ratio:** N/P. **Services for children with learning differences:** N/P. **Policies regarding discipline, drug/alcohol use and abuse prevention and AIDS awareness:** N/P. **Summer programs:** None.

PARENT PARTICIPATION

The school uses volunteers; no minimum number of hours. **Parent education:** "Yes." **Fundraising:** N/P.

What Sets School Apart From Others?

"Catholic community and exciting curriculum."

How Do Parents/Students Characterize the School?

"Fun place to learn; caring community; family feeling."

NUEVA SCHOOL

6565 Skyline Boulevard
Hillsborough, CA 94010
(650) 348-2272 *fax (650) 348-0175*
www.nuevaschool.org

Andrew Beyer, *Executive Director*
Rebecca Hunsiker, *Admissions Director*

We are looking for "bright children who are passionate about learning and who will contribute to our dynamic classrooms." **Our school best serves** "children who love learning, who work well in groups, and are self-directed."

General

Co-ed PreK-8th grade day school. Nonsectarian. Founded 1967. **Nonprofit**, member CAIS, NAIS. **Accreditation**: CAIS/WASC. **Enrollment**: 320. **Average class size**: 16. **Length of school year**: Approximately 180 days. **Length of school day:** 8:35 a.m.-12 p.m. (PreK), 8:35 a.m.-3:20 p.m. (K-8). **Location:** The school is located in Hillsborough, a suburban residential community approximately 18 miles south of San Francisco, approximately one mile from Highway 280.

Student Body

Geographic: Most students come from San Mateo, San Francisco, Burlingame, Portola Valley and other areas of the mid-Peninsula. **Ethnicity:** 78% Caucasian (non-Latino), 7% Asian/Pacific Islander, 6% African-American, 4% Indian. **Foreign students (I-20 status):** None. **Two f/t working parent/single parent families:** N/P.

Admission

<u>Kindergarten</u>. **Application deadline:** Early January (call for exact date). **Age requirement:** For PreK, 4 years old by June 1; for K, 5 years old by September 1. **Application fee:** $180. **Application process:** Includes tour, IQ test, classroom

visit, completed application, school records. **Preschools visited by admission director:** N/P. **Number of applications received:** Approximately 6 applications for each opening. PreK has 18 openings and K has 14. **Preferences:** Siblings. Other grades. Same deadline, admission process and fees. **Test score/GPA cut-off:** N/P. **Estimated number of openings in grades other than K each year:** "Varies."

Costs

Latest tuition: $9,400 for PreK, $13,100 for K-1, $13,400 for G2-3, $14,700 for G4-5, $15,600 for G6, $17,100 for G7-8. **Latest tuition increase:** N/P. **Tuition payment plan:** Available. **Sibling discount:** None. **Percentage of students receiving financial aid:** 20%. **Average grant award:** N/P. **Number of full/partial tuition grants:** N/P.

Program and Philosophy

School's mission statement/goals: "Nueva is a child-centered, Pre-K-8 grade, progressive school for gifted and talented children emphasizing integrated studies, creative arts and social-emotional learning. Our school community inspires passion for lifelong learning, fosters social and emotional acuity and develops the imaginative mind." **Academic program:** "[PreK-G1] are separate classes. [G2-3] combine in mixed age groups to form the Middle Elementary level and [G4-5] combine to form the Upper Elementary level. In the Middle School, [G6-8 students] participate in a grade specific departmentalized curriculum. Subject areas of basic curriculum include language arts, math, social science, computers, science, art, music, library/research skills and P.E. Another component of the curriculum, covering 'process and personal skills' includes critical thinking, creative thinking, problem solving, decision making, leadership and communication skills." **Approach to teaching reading/math:** (Specific approach N/P.) The language arts program emphasizes communication skills and love of literature. **Approach to technology and computer training:** Computer education in grades K-8. Computers are networked. Computer classes are integrated with humanities, science, math, art and music. Keyboarding and computer application skills are also taught. The school uses both PCs and Macs. **Other courses/offerings:** Spanish is offered as an elective in Kindergarten through 8th grade. Japanese is taught as part of the 6-8th grade curriculum, culminating in a trip to Japan at end of 8th grade. Choral singing, visual arts, creative body movement, and drama are also offered. Individual instrumental music instruction is available for an additional fee (scholarships are available through the Menuhin/Dowling Music Scholars Program). Schoolwide there is an emphasis on social emotional learning, leadership skills, and educating the whole child. **Average nightly homework:** Assigned in grades 3-8, ranging from 45 minutes per night in lower grades to about 2-3 hours per night in 7th-8th grades. **Grading system:** "In lieu of traditional grades, Nueva uses extensive written evaluations from the teachers several times a year."

Standardized achievement tests: ERB test administered annually. **Frequency of parent/teacher conferences:** Parent-teacher-child conferences are held at least twice a year. **High schools attended by recent graduates:** Crystal Springs, Menlo, Sacred Heart, University, and Lick. **Other indicators that the school is accomplishing its goals:** N/P.

ATHLETICS

Physical education program: For PreK-5 the program emphasizes cooperation, safety, and trust. Competitive sports are introduced in grades 6-8. **Interscholastic athletics:** The school competes in the Small School Intermediate League in flag football, volleyball, cross-country, basketball and soccer.

FACULTY

Ethnicity, gender breakdown, degrees and credentials: N/P. **Teacher/student ratio:** 8:1. **Faculty selection and professional development:** "The Executive Director and faculty are involved in recruiting, interviewing, and selecting new teachers. Successful candidates must be committed to progressive education and have significant interest in teaching high potential children. The Professional Development budget at Nueva is dedicated to supporting faculty and administrators in their pursuit of graduate study, workshops, training and conferences."

EXTENDED CARE/AFTER-SCHOOL PROGRAMS

Before-school care is provided from 7:30 a.m. to 8:35 a.m. After-school care (supervised study hall or recreational program) is from 3:20 p.m. to 6 p.m. **Cost:** One hour/day is $120 per semester, 2 hours/day is $240, and 3 hours/day is $360. **Drop-in:** Available. **No coverage on:** N/P. **Snacks:** Provided. **Homework:** N/P. **Staff/child ratio:** N/P. **After-school classes:** N/P.

CAMPUS LIFE

Facilities: Situated on a 33-acre campus in Hillsborough, the school has six buildings containing art studios, library, computer lab, new gym, community center (completed March, 2000) and playing field with basketball court and track. The library contains approximately 12,000 volumes. **Meals:** Hot lunch three times a week. **Transportation:** SamTrans bus. **Uniforms:** None. **Co-curricular activities/clubs:** N/P. **Student support services:** Advisory groups in G5-8 and a school therapist. **Services for children with learning differences:** Two learning specialists on staff who work with students in K-8. **Policies regarding discipline, drug/ alcohol use and abuse prevention and AIDS awareness:** The school sponsors health-related programs for middle school students and parents to help educate and to provide a venue for questions and concerns. **Summer program:** Three 2-week summer sessions are offered in July and August. Classes include nature studies, sports, games, art, theater, and animation.

PARENT PARTICIPATION

"We could not do what we do without the tremendous support of our parents."
Parent education: The Parents Association sponsors parent education and coordinates parent representatives who work with teachers and staff to support classroom activities. Literary Club trains and uses approximately 25 parent volunteers each year. **Fundraising:** Coordinated by the development office and Nueva Parents Association.

WHAT SETS SCHOOL APART FROM OTHERS?

"Nueva, a progressive school with a commitment to educating the whole child, is one of the only schools specifically for gifted children in the Bay Area. In addition we emphasize an integrated, hands-on curriculum and everyone at Nueva is on a first name basis."

HOW DO PARENTS/STUDENTS CHARACTERIZE THE SCHOOL?

"Nueva is a dynamic and supportive academic environment that fosters independence."—Parent
"The teachers are great ... and they encourage me to stretch my mind."–Student
"Girls respect boys and boys respect girls and that's why I like Nueva."—Student
"I like Nueva because it allows lots of room for creativity."—Student

ODYSSEY SCHOOL

300 E. Santa Inez
San Mateo, CA 94401
(650) 343-6312 (phone/fax)

Stephen K. Smuin, *Head of School*

We are looking for "creative, gifted/talented students who are intellectually curious, willing to take risks and want to create a community." **Our school best serves** "gifted and talented students."

GENERAL

Co-ed day middle school (grades 6-8). **Nonsectarian.** Founded 1997. **Nonprofit. Accreditation:** "WASC in process." **Enrollment:** 30. **Average class size:** 12. **Length of school year:** 175 days. **Length of school day:** 8:15 a.m.-3:10 p.m. **Location:** In San Mateo, a suburban community approximately 14 miles south of San Francisco. (Nearest cross-street is E. Poplar Avenue.)

STUDENT BODY

Geographic: Students come from San Francisco to Santa Clara. **Ethnicity:** 81% Caucasian (non-Latino), 18% African-American, 1% Asian/Pacific Islander. **Foreign students (I-20 status):** None. **Two f/t working parent families:** 50%. **Single parent families:** 22%.

ADMISSION

Application deadline: Rolling. **Application fee:** $200. **Application process:** Application, testing, visit, interview, portfolio, recommendations, records. Part of the application process requires the applicant to make a presentation from one of the fine or performing arts. **Admission test:** N/P. **Test score/GPA cut-off:** N/P. **Number of applications received:** 22 applications were received last year for 26 spaces. **Preferences:** Siblings are "given consideration."

COSTS

Latest tuition: $13,500. **Last tuition increase:** N/P. **Tuition payment plan:** Available (not specified). **Sibling discount:** None. **Percentage of students receiving financial aid:** 20%. **Average grant award:** $3,500. **Number of full tuition grants:** None. **Number of partial tuition grants:** Four, three of which are half-tuition or more. **Other information regarding financial assistance:** Applicants for financial aid must complete form from ETS and tax return.

PROGRAM AND PHILOSOPHY

School's mission statement/goals. "Odyssey asks every individual to think, question, create and act in an environment of encouragement and compassion, and challenges each person to accept the responsibilities posed by education in a democratic society. Odyssey recognizes that middle school students experience a wide variety of significant social, intellectual, and physical changes and that we must respond and provide for the unique developmental needs and characteristics of these young adolescents." **Academic program and philosophy.** "The Odyssey School Curricular Outline: Connections. The most salient characteristic of the Odyssey course of study is an integrated curriculum. We want students making connections among disciplines, between what is occurring in the real world and their classes, as well as a connection to the real issues in their lives and their course of study. The pedagogy for the curriculum from sixth through eighth grade centers on critical thinking skills, problem solving, cooperative learning groups and a concern with divergent styles of learning and the multiple intelligences. We subscribe to four organizational structures of the curriculum which vary in intensity for each grade level: A. Movement: dance, running, team sports, Tai Chi, stage combat, aerobics and swimming. B. Creative Arts: music history, choir, studio art, art history, photography, film/video, make-up design, set design, costume design. C. Core: Japanese, math, science, writing, humanities. D. Affective Education: Self-Science, advisory, student council, daily gathering, service learning and seminar." **Approach to teaching math/reading:** N/P (middle school). **Approach to technology and computer training:** The school has six computers in its computer lab, four in classrooms. Keyboarding is taught in 6th grade. Computers have Internet access and are available for student use at all times. **Special programs:** Artist-in-Residence—two shows per year. One-week camping trips in fall and spring. One-week trip to Oregon Shakespeare Festival, three-week trip to Japan. **Average nightly homework:** Three hours. **Grading system:** Written evaluations. **Standardized test scores:** Provided to parents (child's own test scores). **Frequency of parent/teacher conferences:** Conferences are held three times/year or as needed. **High schools attended by recent graduates:** Athenian, Menlo, Sacred Heart, University, Lick, Harker, IHS and Crystal Springs. **Other indicators that the school is accomplishing its goals:** "Large number of student body offices held by our graduates."

ATHLETICS

Physical education program: Students participate five times a week; activities include dance, team sports, Tai Chi, aerobics and stage combat. **Interscholastic athletics:** Depends upon the interest of the students.

FACULTY

Gender: 50% male, 50% female. **Ethnicity:** 72% Caucasian (non-Latino), 21% African-American, 7% Latino. **Highest educational degree held:** 80% Bachelor's,

20% Master's. **Credentials:** Four hold California teaching credentials, others hold other credentials and have training in their fields. **Teacher/student ratio:** 1:12. **Faculty training and professional development:** "[E]xtensive paper search, observation, class demonstration, staff interview."

EXTENDED CARE/ AFTER-SCHOOL PROGRAMS

Extended care is available from 3:30 p.m.-5 p.m. for all grades. **Cost:** $4/hour. **Drop-in:** Available. **No coverage on:** Days that school is not in session. **Snacks:** None provided. **Homework:** Homework time is mandatory; assistance "as scheduled." **Staff/child ratio:** 1:6. **After-school classes:** None.

CAMPUS LIFE

Facilities: The school has two buildings on a church property. Facilities include reference room (library), patio, soccer field, gym and pool. **Meals:** None. **Transportation:** No school-sponsored transportation. **Uniforms:** For movement class only. **Co-curricular activities/clubs:** None. **Student support services:** "Support." **Services for children with learning differences:** "Support." **Counselor/ student ratio:** "Advisor/student ratio: 1:6." **Policies regarding drug/alcohol use and abuse prevention and AIDS awareness:** "Zero tolerance." The school also has a health/nutrition education week. **Summer programs:** None.

PARENT PARTICIPATION

"Required." **Parent education:** Parents meet once a month. **Fundraising:** Events include annual giving and fundraising activities.

WHAT SETS SCHOOL APART FROM OTHERS?

"[Odyssey is] the Peninsula's only co-ed private school for gifted and talented students."

HOW DO PARENTS/STUDENTS CHARACTERIZE THE SCHOOL?

"A community."

THE PHILLIPS BROOKS SCHOOL

2245 Avy Avenue
Menlo Park, CA 94025
(650) 854-4545 *fax (650) 854-6532*
www.phillipsbrooks.pvt.k12.ca.us

Beth Passi, *Head of School*
Clair Ward, *Assistant Head of School*

[Ed. Note: This profile is based on a visit to the school and the school's printed materials, including its annual report, admissions packet and newsletter.]

GENERAL

Co-ed Preschool-5th grade day school. Nonsectarian. Founded 1978. **Non-profit**, member NAIS/CAIS. **Accreditation:** CAIS. **Enrollment**: 230. **Average class size:** Ranges between 12-15 (preschool), 18 (K-2) and 24 (grades 3-5). **Length of school day:** N/P. **Length of school year:** N/P. **Location:** In a Menlo Park residential neighborhood, north of Sand Hill Road and west of the Alameda de las Pulgas. (Note: The school has recently purchased 92 acres of land in Woodside for construction of a new campus.)

STUDENT BODY

Geographic: N/P. (Most students come from nearby communities, including Menlo Park, Atherton, Woodside and Portola Valley.) **Ethnicity:** N/P. **Foreign students:** N/P. **Two f/t working parent families:** N/P. **Single parent families:** N/P.

ADMISSION

<u>Kindergarten</u>. **Application deadline:** Return form "as soon as possible," no later than late February (check with school for date). **Age requirement:** N/P. (Child must be age 3 by September 1 to enter the Early Learning Center 3-year-olds program, so those children will be age 5 by September 1 of their Kindergarten year.) **Application fee:** $55. **Application process:** Complete forms, including teacher recommendation form, attend tour, schedule classroom visit (for prospective parents), screening in January - March. Criteria for admission: "A correlation between the school's philosophy and the goals for the child's parents, learning style and aptitude, developmental readiness or academic achievement, social-emotional development, motivation, [and] the ability of the School to meet the needs of the child." **Preschools visited by admission director:** N/P. **Number of applications received:** N/P. **Preferences:** N/P. **Other grades.** Same as above, with testing on a Saturday morning in January or March. **Admission test:** N/P. **Test score/GPA cut-off:** N/P. **Estimated number of openings in grades other**

than K each year: N/P. "We are looking for ..." N/P. "Our school best serves ..." N/P.

COSTS

Latest tuition: $10,070 for K, $11,160 for grades 1-5. **Last tuition increase:** N/P. **Tuition payment plan:** N/P. **Sibling discount:** N/P. **Financial aid:** [Ed. Note: According to a recent annual report, the school budgeted approximately $200,000 for financial aid.] **Other information regarding financial assistance:** "The school must receive an application for admission before a financial aid package can be mailed. Call the school office as soon as possible if you are interested in receiving a financial aid application. The financial aid application process must be initiated early in order for Phillips Brooks to receive the necessary materials from the School and Student Service in Princeton, New Jersey by [the admission application deadline]."

PROGRAM AND PHILOSOPHY

School philosophy. "Our objective is to prepare each student to live a creative, humane and compassionate life and to be a contributing member of society. The spiritual growth of the child is integrated into every aspect of The Phillips Brooks School educational process. We foster spiritual and moral values by example as well as through the curriculum and community service. Children are taught to show respect for themselves, for others and for the environment. We seek to have students solve problems through open communication. We encourage students to reach beyond themselves, to value and embrace cultural, ethnic and socioeconomic diversity, and to respond to the needs and rights of everyone." **Academic program. Approach to teaching math/reading:** N/P. **Approach to technology and computer training:** The school has computer lab and a technology coordinator. All classrooms have Internet access. Computer activities are integrated with the curriculum and include weather units in lower grades and multimedia projects about California missions in 4th grade. Keyboarding is taught in 3rd grade. **Other courses/offerings:** Foreign languages (French and Spanish); specialized teachers provide additional instruction in art, science, music, computer, library and physical education. **Special programs:** California missions (4th grade), outdoor education (Grade 5), chapel program, School Bee, Christmas pageant, spring musical. **Grading system:** N/P. **Frequency of parent/teacher conferences:** N/P. **Standardized test scores:** Test results are sent to parents, and the school shares its overall performance with the school community. **Middle schools attended by recent graduates:** Many of the area's middle and high schools, including Menlo, Castilleja, Crystal Springs and Woodside Priory. **Other indicators that the school is accomplishing its goals:** N/P.

ATHLETICS

Physical education program: "Taught by a specialist." **Interscholastic sports:** N/P.

FACULTY

Gender: 88% female, 12% male. **Ethnicity:** N/P. **Highest educational degree held:** Approximately 1/3 of faculty hold advanced degrees. **Credentials:** N/P. **Teacher/student ratio:** 1:10. **Faculty training and professional development:** N/P.

EXTENDED CARE/AFTER-SCHOOL PROGRAMS

N/P.

PINEWOOD

327 Fremont Avenue
Los Altos, CA 94024
(650) 941-2828 *fax (650) 941-2459*

Alice Johnson, *Principal*

GENERAL

Co-ed K-6 day school (with grades 7-12 on a separate campus). **Nonsectarian.** Founded 1959. **Nonprofit. Accreditation:** N/P. **Enrollment:** 300. **Average class size:** 16. **Length of school year:** 175 days. **Length of school day:** 8:30 a.m.-3 p.m. (lower school), 8:30 a.m.-3:15 p.m. (middle school). **Location:** Located in a residential area adjacent to Los Altos Hills, accessible from Highway 280 and Foothill Expressway.

STUDENT BODY

Geographic: N/P. **Ethnicity:** N/P. **Foreign students (I-20 status):** N/P. **Two f/t working parent/single parent families:** N/P.

ADMISSION

Kindergarten. Application deadline: Early February (call for exact date). **Age requirement:** N/P. **Application fee:** $50. **Application process:** Test and interview. **Preschools visited by admission director:** N/P. **Number of applications received:** 150 applications received for 48 spaces in latest K class. **Preferences:** Siblings. **Other grades. Application deadline:** Early February (call for exact date). **Application fee:** $50. **Application process:** Test and interview. (Type of test: N/P). **Test score/GPA cut-off:** N/P. **Estimated number of openings in grades other than K each year:** "Varies year to year, but we have a very limited number of opening each year." **"We are looking for ..."** N/P. **"Our school best serves ..."** N/P.

Costs

Latest tuition: $6,200 for K, $8,800 for G1-6, and $10,100 for G7-8. **Last tuition increase:** N/P. **Tuition payment plan:** Monthly, yearly, or semi-monthly. **Sibling discount:** None. **Financial aid:** None.

Program and Philosophy

School's mission statement/goals. "Pinewood is a college preparatory school. It is designed to provide a positive learning climate in which students develop academic stamina, intellectual vitality, and a high standard of behavior. This training will enable students to fulfill a life of purpose, dignity, self-esteem and concern for others." **Academic program. Approach to teaching reading:** N/P. **Approach to teaching math:** N/P. **Approach to technology and computer training:** N/P. **Other courses/offerings:** French (grades 1-6), art, music (choral), and athletics. **Special programs:** Field trips, drama, outdoor education and overnight trips. **Average nightly homework:** N/P. **Grading system:** N/P. **Frequency of parent/teacher conferences:** Regular bulletins; conferences upon request. **Standardized test scores:** N/P. **High schools attended by recent graduates:** N/P (Pinewood has a high school program). **Other indicators that the school is accomplishing its goals:** N/P.

Athletics

Physical education program: "Full-time P.E. teacher." **Interscholastic athletics:** None in grades K-6. Introduced at grade 7-8 level. Other: Weekly after-school sports programs.

Faculty

Gender: 85% female, 15% male. **Ethnicity:** N/P. **Highest educational degree held:** Bachelor's 70%, Master's 23%, Doctorate 7%. **Credentials:** N/P. **Teacher/ student ratio:** 1:10. **Faculty training and professional development:** "We look at teaching experience and educational background."

Extended Care/After-School Programs

Daily after-school care provided from 3:30 p.m.-5:45 p.m. **Cost:** N/P. **Drop-in:** N/P. **No coverage on:** N/P. **Snacks:** Provided. **Homework:** Required. **Staff/child ratio:** N/P. **After-school classes:** For a fee, after-school clubs are offered, such as sports club, science club, performing arts club, and art club.

Campus Life

Facilities: The school has three campuses: a lower campus housing K-2, a middle campus for G3-6 in a renovated residence in Los Altos, and, in Los Altos Hills, a large (7-acre) upper campus for G7-12. **Meals:** "Available." **Transportation:** No school-sponsored transportation. **Uniforms:** Required. **Co-curricular activities/clubs:** Yes. **Student support services:** N/P. **Services for children with learning differences:** None. **Counselor/student ratio:** N/P. **Policies regarding discipline, drug/alcohol use and abuse and AIDS awareness:** N/P. **Summer programs:** Yes (cost N/P).

PARENT PARTICIPATION

N/P. **Parent education:** N/P. **Fundraising:** None.

WHAT SETS SCHOOL APART FROM OTHERS?

"We are departmentalized in grades K-12. A student will have a teacher who specializes in his or her field, meaning they will have 6-7 different teachers in one day rather than having one teacher who teaches all subjects."

HOW DO PARENTS/STUDENTS CHARACTERIZE THE SCHOOL?

"They love the school. The students work hard and play hard, and they progress to leading colleges across the nation. We are one big Pinewood family."

QUEEN OF APOSTLES

4950 Mitty Way
San Jose, CA 95129
(408) 252-3659 *fax (408) 873-2645*
www.qofa.org

Marianna Willis, *Principal*

GENERAL

Co-ed K-8 Catholic parochial school (% Catholic N/P). Founded 1964. **Accreditation:** WASC (6-year term). **Enrollment:** 315. **Average class size:** 35. **Length of school year:** 180 days. **Length of school day:** 8 a.m.-2:40 p.m. **Location:** Off Lawrence Expressway near Highway 280

STUDENT BODY

Geographic: Most students come from San Jose and Cupertino. **Ethnicity:** 82% Caucasian (non-Latino), 8% Latino, 6% Asian/Pacific Islander, 1% Middle Eastern or East Indian, 1% Filipino, <1% African-American, <1% other. **Foreign students (I-20 status):** None. **Two f/t working parent families:** 74%. **Single parent families:** 26%.

ADMISSION

Kindergarten. Application deadline: "Before screening in March." **Age requirement:** 5 years old by December 1. **Application fee:** $10. **Application process:** All applicants go through developmental screening. **Preschools visited by admission director:** N/P. **Number of applications received:** N/P. **Preferences:** Siblings. **Other grades. Application deadline:** Before March screening. **Application fee:** $10. **Application process:** Language arts, math testing. **Admission test:** Given in early March (N/P which test). **Test score/GPA cut-off:** N/P. **Estimated number of openings in grades other than K each year:** "Varies." **"We are looking for ..."** N/P. **"Our school best serves ..."** N/P.

COSTS

Latest tuition: $3,319 for in-parish, $3,810 for all others. **Last tuition increase:** Approximately 10%. **Sibling discount:** 20% off for 2nd child, 51% off for 3rd. N/P.

PROGRAM AND PHILOSOPHY

N/P.

FACULTY

Gender: 88% female, 12% male. **Ethnicity:** 100% Caucasian (non-Latino). **Highest educational degree held:** "Some teachers hold Master's degrees." **Credentials:** 99% of teachers have California teaching credentials, 1% have other credential. **Teacher/student ratio:** 2:35 lower school, 1:35 middle school. **Faculty selection and professional development:** The school has in-service programs for teachers.

EXTENDED CARE/AFTER-SCHOOL PROGRAMS

Extended care is available from 6:30 a.m. to 7:45 a.m. and after dismissal until 6 p.m. **Cost:** $174/month. **Drop in:** Available. **No coverage on:** School holidays and summer vacation. **Snacks:** Provided. **Homework:** Time provided. **Staff/child ratio:** "Varies." **After-school classes:** Spanish and music.

CAMPUS LIFE

N/P. The school is next to Archbishop Mitty High School, a large (1,430-student) co-ed Catholic high school.

PARENT PARTICIPATION

N/P.

What Sets School Apart From Others?

N/P.

How Do Parents/Students Characterize the School?

N/P.

REDEEMER LUTHERAN SCHOOL

468 Grand Street
Redwood City, CA 94062
(650) 366-3466 *fax (650) 366-5898*

Gary Behrens, *Principal* (gbehrens@recochet.net)

We are looking for "willing learners and supportive parents." **Our school best serves** "children who love learning."

GENERAL

Co-ed K-8 Lutheran school (45% of students are Lutheran). Founded 1957. **Accreditation:** WASC (through 2001) and National Lutheran Schools Accreditation (through 2002). **Enrollment:** 180. **Average class size:** 24. **Length of school year:** 181 days. **Length of school day:** 8:30 a.m.-3 p.m. **Location:** Redwood City, west of El Camino Real and north of Jefferson Avenue

STUDENT BODY

Geographic: Most students come from Redwood City, San Carlos and Menlo Park. **Ethnicity:** 84% Caucasian (non-Latino), 7% Latino, 4% African-American, 3% Asian/Pacific Islander, 2% Middle Eastern or East Indian. **Foreign students (I-20 status):** None. **Two f/t working/single parent families:** N/P.

ADMISSION

Kindergarten. **Application deadline:** Beginning February 1. **Age requirement:** 5 years old by December 1. **Application fee:** $250 total. **Application process:** Submit $100 and application, followed by 1 hour of one-on-one screening plus 2.5 hours in a group setting. **Preschools visited by admission director:** N/P. **Preferences:** Siblings, church members. **Other grades. Application deadline:** N/A. **Application fee:** $250. **Application process:** Depends upon completeness of current records. Students who have been expelled from their previous school will not be eligible for enrollment. **Admission test:** N/P. **Test score/GPA cut-off:** N/P. **Estimated number of openings in grades other than K each year:** "Varies from 2 to 5."

COSTS

Latest tuition: $3,925. **Last tuition increase:** Less than 10%. **Tuition payment plan:** 10-payment plan available. **Sibling discount:** Approximately $350/year. **Percentage of students receiving financial aid:** 15%. **Average grant award:** $500. **Number of full tuition grants:** None. **Number of partial tuition grants:** Three, all of which were half-tuition or more. **Other information regarding financial assistance:** "Families should apply annually, prior to June. [Awards are] based on income."

PROGRAM AND PHILOSOPHY

School's mission statement/goals. "Redeemer Lutheran Elementary School (Grades K-8), focusing on the greater Redwood City community, is a place where teachers, parents and congregation members work together to share the Good News of salvation, nurturing children with God's love and grace. Our primary goal is to help children develop a positive view of the future and acquire the attitudes, knowledge and skills necessary to become successful, contributing Christians in a rapidly changing world." **Academic program.** Teaching strategies include: "Liberal use of 'hands-on'/multi-media activities, the development of critical thinking skills, learning cooperative group skills, selecting appropriate field trips and assemblies. The school community provides a learning environment where children are successful both as individuals and group members. Learning strategies emphasize both individual and cooperative group skills. Teachers use peer tutoring as a means to build self-esteem. Teachers cooperate by providing opportunities for older students to work with younger students." **Approach to teaching reading:** Phonics-based. **Approach to teaching math:** N/P. **Approach to technology and computer training:** "Computers are in classrooms of grades 4-8; technology is integrated into curriculum; lab for K-3. Keyboarding starts in grade 1." **Other courses/offerings:** Spanish, art, music (choir for grades 4-8, instrumental music by private lesson), athletics (grades 5-8). **Special programs:** Drama, outdoor education, Sacramento field trips and Washington, D.C. field trip in 8th grade. **Average nightly homework:** 1-2 hours. **Grading system for grades K-2:** R, G and C (for "Rarely," "Generally" and "Consistently"). **Grading system for grades 3-8:** A-F. **Frequency of parent/teacher conferences:** Parent/teacher conferences at 1st, 2nd, 3rd quarter. Weekly class newsletter, monthly school newsletter. **Standardized test scores:** Provided to parents (child's scores, school community, school's overall performance), prospective parents and anyone else who asks. **High schools attended by most recent graduates:** Menlo-Atherton (public) (1), St. Francis (1), Mercy (2), Woodside (public) (4), Serra (2) and Sequoia (public) (5). **Other indicators that the school is accomplishing its goals:** "Standardized test scores, word-of-mouth recommendations."

ATHLETICS

Physical education program: Consists of a prescribed program taught by classroom teachers. **Interscholastic athletics:** The school competes with other Lutheran schools in grades 5-8 in volleyball and basketball. Track meet for grades K-8.

FACULTY

Gender: 67.5% female, 37.5% male. **Ethnicity:** 100% Caucasian. **Highest educational degree held:** 75% Bachelor's, 25% Master's. **Credentials:** Four teachers have California teaching credentials, two have other credentials or training. **Teacher/student ratio:** 1:24. **Faculty selection and professional development:** The school conducts a search and interview process. The minimum educational requirement is a bachelor's degree.

EXTENDED CARE/AFTER-SCHOOL PROGRAMS

Extended care is available mornings from 7 a.m. and after school until 5:45 p.m. for grades K-6. **Cost:** Varies from $50/month for a.m. only to $200 for a.m. and p.m. **Drop-in:** None. **No coverage on:** National holidays. **Snacks:** Provided. **Homework:** Homework time is mandatory and staff provides assistance. **Staff/child ratio:** 1:22. **After school classes:** Karate.

CAMPUS LIFE

Facilities: The church and school occupy half a city block. The school has a small library. **Meals:** Hot lunches are provided 3-4 days/week. **Transportation:** N/P. **Uniforms:** Required. **Co-curricular activities/clubs:** Variety, determined annually. **Student support services:** Screening, testing and tutoring. Hearing and vision screening. **Services for children with learning differences:** Tutoring. **Counselor/student ratio:** None. **Policies regarding discipline, drug/alcohol use and abuse prevention and AIDS awareness:** N/P (described in school handbook). **Summer program:** None.

PARENT PARTICIPATION

35 hours required of 2-parent families, 10 hours for single parents. **Parent education:** 3-4 classes per year. **Fundraising:** Scrip sales, gift-wrap sales, hot lunch.

WHAT SETS SCHOOL APART FROM OTHERS?

"Parent support, peer coaching, sports program, high academics."

HOW DO PARENTS/STUDENTS CHARACTERIZE THE SCHOOL?

"Solid, caring staff, family atmosphere, fun."

ST. CATHERINE OF SIENA SCHOOL

1300 Bayswater Avenue
Burlingame, CA 94010
(650) 344-7176 *fax (650) 344-7426*

Sr. Teresa Pallitto, *Principal*

We are looking for "families committed to Catholic education. We want every-one to understand that we are a parish school and a commitment to the school is a commitment to the parish." **Our school best serves** "those families who realize that Catholic education is based on collaboration—collaboration with God's grace and with the whole community."

General

Co-ed K-8 Catholic parochial school (88% of students are Catholic). Founded in 1938. **Nonprofit. Accreditation**: WASC/WCEA. **Enrollment**: 324. **Average class size**: 36. **Length of school year**: 180 days. **Length of school day:** 8:25 a.m.-3 p.m. **Location:** In Burlingame, a suburban community approximately 16 miles south of San Francisco. Bayswater is east of El Camino and north of Penin-sula Avenue.

Student Body

Geographic: Most students come from Burlingame, San Mateo, and Foster City. **Ethnicity:** 61% Caucasian, 15% multi-racial, 9% Asian/Pacific Islander, 8% Fili-pino, 5% Latino, 1% Native American, 1% African-American. **Foreign students (I-20 status):** None. **Two f/t working parent families:** 48%. **Single parent families:** 12%.

ADMISSION

Kindergarten. Application deadline December 31. **Age requirement:** 5 years old before December 1 (of Kindergarten year). **Application fee:** None. **Application process:** Application, family interview, school readiness test. **Preschools visited by admission director:** N/P. **Number of applications received:** 76 applications received last year for 22 spaces. No preschool on campus. **Preferences:** Siblings, alumni, and active parishioners. **Other grades. Application deadline:** March (check with school for date). **Application fee:** None. **Application process:** Application, testing, interview with family upon acceptance. **Test score/GPA cut-off:** None. **Estimated number of openings in grades other than K each year:** "Varies."

COSTS

Latest tuition: $2,908 for parish member, $3,625 for out-of-parish Catholics. **Last tuition increase:** N/P. **Tuition payment plan:** Available. **Sibling discount:** Yes. **Percentage of students receiving financial aid:** 15% of families. **Average grant award:** $1,381. **Number of full tuition grants:** One. **Number of partial tuition grants:** 32, all of which are half-tuition or more. **Other information regarding financial assistance:** "St. Catherine of Siena School offers assistance to families of need."

PROGRAM AND PHILOSOPHY

School's mission statement/goals. "St. Catherine of Siena School is committed to a Catholic education in which the faith experience and academic excellence empower the student to live out the Gospel message." **Academic goals:** "To strive for academic excellence while emphasizing a comprehensive and sequential curriculum and encouraging the achievement of a student's full potential; to develop critical and evaluative thinking skills in all areas of the curriculum; to recognize multiple intelligences and teach accordingly, thereby promoting improvement, growth and success for all students; to enrich the general curriculum with various activities that will generate curiosity and creativity allowing the students to discover and develop aptitudes; to create opportunities for cultural awareness; to evaluate the academic program, to assess student learning, and to update curriculum, materials, methodology, and technology." **Academic program. Approach to teaching reading:** "Whole language-literature based, but incorporated with traditional English, spelling and phonics programs." **Approach to teaching math:** N/P. **Approach to technology and computer training:** The school has a computer lab, which students use once a week. The school is working on obtaining classroom computers. No Internet access yet. **Other courses/offerings:** Spanish or Italian, art, music instruction, and athletics (K-8). **Special programs:** Outdoor education (grade 5), educational field studies in Monterey, Sacramento, and San Francisco (grade 8), Days of Recollection (grade 7-8), sacramental program (grade 2), Burlingame Police Department G.R.E.A.T. Program (grade 3 and 7). **Average nightly homework:** As established by Archdiocesan guidelines,

10-20 minutes for K, 20-30 minutes for grades 1-2, 30-40 minutes for grades 3-4, 45-60 minutes for grades 5-6, and 60-90 minutes for grades 7-8. (7th and 8th graders sometimes have weekend homework.) **Grading system:** Kindergarten program uses "Very Good," "Good" and "Satisfactory." All other grades receive letter grades (A-F). **Frequency of parent/teacher conferences:** "Official conferences annually but teachers are readily available upon the request of parent." **Standardized test scores:** Provided to parents (child's scores) and school community (school's overall performance). **High schools attended by recent graduates:** St. Ignatius (7), Notre Dame (6), Mercy (6), Serra (5), and Sacred Heart (1). **Other indicators that the school is accomplishing its goals:** "Happy students, warm faculty, supportive parish."

ATHLETICS

Physical education program: Instructional services provided by Rhythm and Moves. **Interscholastic sports:** The school participates in the PPSL. Boys compete in baseball, basketball and track. Girls compete in volleyball, basketball, and track and may participate in cheerleading.

FACULTY

Gender: 95% female, 5% male. **Ethnicity:** 81% Caucasian (non-Latino), 9% multi-racial, 5% Latino, 5% Filipino. **Highest educational degree held:** Bachelor's 40%, Master's 28%. **Credentials:** N/P. Some teachers have "special education/administrative" training. **Teacher/student ratio:** 1:36. **Faculty selection and professional development:** "Archdiocese screens applicants first. They are chosen after an interview based on how they could live the philosophy of the school. Teachers are encouraged to continually update."

EXTENDED CARE/AFTER-SCHOOL PROGRAMS

Extended care is offered after school only, from dismissal (12:45 p.m. or 3 p.m.) until 6 p.m. **Cost:** $2.50/hour per child. **Drop-in:** Available. **No coverage on:** Holidays such as the day before Thanksgiving and Christmas vacation. **Snacks:** Provided. **Homework:** Must be done in extended care. **Staff/child ratio:** 2:25. **After-school classes:** None.

CAMPUS LIFE

Facilities: The campus buildings, as well as the St. Catherine of Siena Church, are Gothic style. Nine spacious classrooms are located on two floors of the school building. The library, which houses approximately 2,000 volumes, is visited weekly by classes. **Meals:** Hot lunch twice a week; milk daily if ordered. **Transportation:** N/A. **Uniforms:** Skirt or pants for girls with white blouse; pants and white shirts for boys. Uniform shorts are optional. **Co-curricular activities/clubs:** Student government, student council and school newspaper. **Student support services:** Hearing screening in grades 4 and 7, vision screening in grades 1-8, counseling.

Services for children with learning differences: "Resource specialist on staff - try to meet the needs of all." **Policies regarding discipline, drug/alcohol use and abuse prevention and AIDS awareness:** "Discipline is handled primarily by the classroom teacher. The principal assists when requested. Drug/alcohol abuse prevention and AIDS awareness is part of the 8th grade science curriculum." **Summer program:** None.

PARENT PARTICIPATION

"The school relies upon parent involvement. 40 hours per year is obligatory for all families." **Parent education:** "Some workshops provided." **Fundraising:** Major fundraisers are the Parish Festival, scrip program ($300/family/month), chocolate sales, book fair and spell-a-thon.

WHAT SETS SCHOOL APART FROM OTHERS?

"The positive climate and strong sense of community where everyone generally seeks the good of the other."

HOW DO PARENTS/STUDENT CHARACTERIZE THE SCHOOL?

"Friendly, academically challenging, strong religious formation, good reputation."

ST. CHARLES SCHOOL

850 Tamarack Avenue
San Carlos, CA 94070
(650) 593-1629 *fax (650) 593-9723*
stchassncrls@impresso.com

Arlene B. Weidner, *Principal*
Kevin R. Oliver, *Vice Principal*

GENERAL

Co-ed K-8 Catholic parochial school (98% of students are Catholic). Founded 1950. **Nonprofit. Accreditation:** WASC/WCEA (6-year accreditation). **Enrollment:** 315. **Average class size:** 35. **Length of school year:** 181 days. **Length of school day:** 8:12 a.m.-3 p.m. **Location:** In San Carlos, a suburban community approximately 20 miles south of San Francisco. Tamarack is east of Alameda de las Pulgas, west of El Camino.

STUDENT BODY

Geographic: Most students come from the communities of San Carlos, Redwood City, Belmont and San Mateo. **Ethnicity:** 95% Caucasian (non-Latino), 4% Latino, 1% other. **Foreign students (I-20 status):** None. **Two f/t working parent families:** Approx. 75%. **Single parent families:** Approx. 11%.

ADMISSION

<u>Kindergarten.</u> **Application deadline** February 1. **Age requirement:** 5 years old by September 1. **Application fee:** None; $40 testing fee. **Application process:** Completed application, letter of recommendation, testing and interview. **Preschools visited by admission director:** N/P. **Number of applications received:** 110 spaces received last year for 40 spaces (36 K, 4 other grades). **Preferences:** Siblings, active parish members. <u>**Other grades.**</u> **Application deadline:** March 1. **Application fee:** None; $40 testing fee. **Application process:** (same as above). Admission test administered in March. **Test score/GPA cut-off:** None. **Estimated number of openings in grades other than K each year:** 5 to 8. **"We are looking for ..."** N/P. **"Our school best serves ..."** N/P.

COSTS

Latest tuition: Approximately $3,212 for one child (in-parish), $3,462 for non-participating Catholics. **Last tuition increase:** Approximately 3-5% per year. **Tuition payment plan:** 1-, 2-, 10- or 12-payment plan available. **Sibling discount:** $50 per child. **Percentage of students receiving financial aid:** 3%. **Average grant award:** $1,000. **Number of full tuition grants:** Two. **Number of partial tuition grants:** 8. **Other information regarding financial assistance:** Financial assistance is also available through programs of the Archdiocese. "Endowment fund in place; development is ongoing."

PROGRAM AND PHILOSOPHY

<u>School's mission statement/goals</u>. "St. Charles is a Catholic parish school dedicated to providing a safe and nurturing environment for students. The faculty, in partnership with the parents, promotes a community of faith and endeavors to challenge students to reach their fullest potential. Inspired by Jesus' life, students are encouraged to become participating members of the Church and world community as they prepare to enter the twenty-first century." [Academic philosophy:] "St. Charles School strives to recognize individual differences and talents, develop students' potential and instill each with a desire to pursue life-long learning." **Academic program. Approach to teaching reading:** Traditional phonics-based approach that includes much literature and creative writing. **Approach to teaching math:** Traditional with use of manipulatives. **Approach to technology and computer training:** "The school has a computer lab with 18 computers and various peripheral equipment with a full-time instructor. Keyboarding is taught beginning in 4th grade through a keyboarding program. We are networked with

Internet access. Lab is open 2 days a week after school and at lunchtime as needed."
Other courses/offerings Music (choral, grades K-8), athletics, library program
for grades K-6. **Special programs:** Outdoor education (Walden West in grade 6,
Caritas Creek in grade 8). ROPES program in grade 8, Junior High Science-
Velocity Workshop at Great America. **Average nightly homework:** 20 minutes
for K-2, 30-45 minutes for grades 3-4, 45-60 minutes for grades 5-6, and 60-90
minutes for grades 7-8. **Grading system for lower school:** S or S- (K), P or N
(Grades 1-3). **Grading system for middle school:** Grades 4-8 receive letter grades
(A-F). **Frequency of parent/teacher conferences:** One formal conference/year;
8 progress reports throughout year. Weekly family envelope to inform parents of
school events and activities. **Standardized test scores:** Provided to parents (child's
own scores) and school community (school's overall performance). **High schools
attended by recent graduates:** Notre Dame (14), Serra (10), St. Ignatius (3),
Mercy (3), Bellarmine (1), Carlmont (1), S.F. School of Performing Arts (1), St.
Francis (1). **Other indicators the school is accomplishing its goals:** "Alumni
and parent feedback."

ATHLETICS

Physical education program: Each grade receives 45-60 minutes of instruction
per week. The school has a gym and a P.E. instructor. **Interscholastic athletics:**
The school competes in the Peninsula Parochial School League. Boys may participate in baseball (grades 4-8), basketball (grades 4-8), and track (grades 5-8).
Girls may participate in basketball (grades 4-8), volleyball (grades 4-8), track
(grades 5-8) and cheerleading (grade 8).

FACULTY

Gender: 67% female, 13% male. **Ethnicity:** 100% Caucasian (non-Latino). **Highest educational degree held:** Bachelor's 60%, Master's 40%. **Credentials:** 80%
hold California teaching credentials, 20% hold other credentials or have training. **Teacher/student ratio:** 1:35. **Faculty training and professional development:** "Teachers are selected based on credentials and recommendations. Teachers are required to participate in in-service programs and updating to maintain
status on pay scale."

EXTENDED CARE/AFTER-SCHOOL PROGRAMS

Extended care is available from 7 a.m. until class begins and after school until
6 p.m. for grades K-8. **Cost:** $3.25/hour and $25 registration fee. **Drop-in:** Available. **No coverage on:** Days when school is not in session. **Snacks:** Provided.
Homework: Homework time is voluntary; assistance is available from staff and a
Homework Club teacher. Computer lab is also available 2 days a week. **Staff/
child ratio:** 1:18. **After-school classes:** Classes include Science Club ($45 per
session) and Irish Step Dancing ($45 per month).

Campus Life

Facilities: The school is in one building "in the shape of a tuning fork." N/P re library. **Meals:** Available Tuesday, Wednesday and Thursday. **Transportation:** No school-sponsored transportation. **Uniforms:** Required. **Co-curricular activities/clubs:** Student council, yearbook club and Holy Childhood Association. **Student support services:** Extended care program, vision/hearing/scoliosis screenings, D.A.R.E. program, and educational testing. **Services for children with learning differences:** Resource teacher for grades K-4. **Counselor/student ratio:** 1:315. **Policies regarding discipline, drug/alcohol use and abuse prevention and AIDS awareness:** "All areas are taught based on Archdiocesan guidelines." **Summer programs:** Summer school is available for grades K-5; approximate cost is $265.

Parent Participation

"Parent volunteers are used in classrooms, for traffic supervision, lunch room servers, fund raising, maintenance projects, etc." 40 hours are required of 2-parent families, 20 hours of single-parent families. **Parent education:** Speakers are provided 2-3 times/year to discuss parent education issues. **Fundraising:** Parish carnival, school auction, and gift wrap sales. No contribution required.

What Sets School Apart From Others?

"Dedicated faculty and staff; informed parent community; caring community."

How Do Parents/Students Characterize the School?

"St. Charles offers an excellent education in a community where commitment to Christian values and morals is supported by a dedicated staff in a safe and nurturing environment."

ST. GREGORY

2701 Hacienda St.
San Mateo, CA 94403
(650) 573-0111 *fax (650) 573-6548*
www.stgregs-sanmateo.org
stgregsm@impresso.com

Patricia Teilh, *Principal and Head of Admissions*

We are looking for "Catholic, Christian children who have parents active within their parish." **Our school best serves** "the needs of our Church."

GENERAL

Co-ed PreK-8 Catholic parochial school (98% of students are Catholic). Founded 1954. **Nonprofit. Accreditation:** WASC/WCEA. **Enrollment:** 318. **Average class size:** 36. **Length of school year:** 180 days. **Length of school day:** 8:15 a.m.-3 p.m. **Location:** In San Mateo, 20 miles south of San Francisco, between El Camino and Alameda de las Pulgas, south of Highway 92.

STUDENT BODY

Geographic: Most students come from San Mateo. **Ethnicity:** 82% Caucasian, 8% Asian/Pacific Islander, 8% Filipino, 1% Latino, 1% African-American. **Foreign students:** None. **Two f/t working parent families:** 90%. **Single parent families:** 10%.

ADMISSION

Kindergarten. Application deadline: January 29 (check with school for date for current year). **Age requirement:** 5 years old by December 1. **Application fee:** $25 testing fee. **Application process:** N/P. **Preschools visited by admission director:** N/P. **Number of applications received:** 60 applications received last year for 36 spaces; 34 spaces filled by school's own preschool students. **Preferences:** Siblings, active parishioners. **Other grades. Application deadline:** March 15. **Application fee:** $25 testing fee. **Application process:** Testing. **Test score/ GPA cut-off:** None. **Estimated number of openings in grades other than K each year:** 5.

COSTS

Latest tuition: Approximately $2,600. **Last tuition increase:** Approximately 4%. **Tuition payment plan:** Monthly plan available. **Sibling discount:** None. **Percentage of students receiving financial aid:** 10%. **Average grant award:** $500. **Number of full tuition grants:** None. **Number of partial tuition grants:** 15, all for half-tuition or more.

PROGRAM AND PHILOSOPHY

School's mission statement/goals. "St. Gregory School nurtures the spiritual, physical, emotional, intellectual, and social development of each student. In the spirit of Jesus, we are committed to teaching and living Gospel values within our Christian community and the world around us. We teach to Catholic values and to our school philosophy." **Approach to teaching reading:** Whole language. **Approach to teaching math:** Concepts, computation, thought process. **Approach to technology and computer training:** "We use the computer as a tool for integrated study. We have 20 computers in a lab with a computer teacher. Computers are also in classrooms." **Other courses/offerings** Art, drama, instrumental music (after school for additional fee), and athletics. **Special programs:** Drama, outdoor education (6th grade), Yosemite trip (8th grade). **Average nightly homework:** 1.5 to 3 hours (Mon.-Thurs.). **Grading system:** N/P. **Frequency of parent/teacher conferences:** Fall quarter and whenever necessary. **Standardized test scores:** Provided to parents (child's own scores) and school community (school's overall performance). **High schools attended by recent graduates:** Serra, Notre Dame, St. Ignatius, Mercy, Hillsdale (public), Aragon (public). **Other indicators that the school is accomplishing its goals:** "35 out of 36 graduates attend Catholic high schools."

ATHLETICS

Physical education program: "Goals meet Archdiocesan guidelines. We have one instructor with wonderful facilities including a gym." **Interscholastic athletics:** 4th-8th grade girls and boys participate in the Archdiocesan league.

FACULTY

Gender: 92% female, 8% male. **Ethnicity:** 100% Caucasian (non-Latino). **Highest educational degree held:** 96% Bachelor's, 4% Master's. **Credentials:** All have California teaching credentials. **Teacher/student ratio:** 2:36 (lower school), 1:36 (middle school). **Faculty training and professional development:** "Interview process by selection committee, mandatory professional growth paid by school at rate of $500 per year per teacher."

EXTENDED CARE/AFTER-SCHOOL PROGRAMS

Extended care is available from 7 a.m. to 8 a.m. and from 3 p.m. to 6 p.m. **Cost:** $3.50/hour. **Drop-in:** Available. **No coverage on:** School holidays. **Snacks:** Provided. **Homework:** Homework time is mandatory and assistance is provided. **Staff/child ratio:** 3:10. **After-school classes:** None.

CAMPUS LIFE

Facilities: The school occupies one square block and has five buildings. N/P re library. **Meals:** Hot lunch three times per week. **Transportation:** No school-sponsored transportation. **Uniforms:** Required. **Co-curricular activities/clubs:** N/P. **Student support services:** Catholic Charities counselor. **Services for children with learning differences:** "Limited." **Counselor/student ratio:** 1:25. **Policies regarding discipline, drug/alcohol use and abuse prevention and AIDS awareness:** Individual programs address all issues. **Summer programs:** $290 for 3-week session.

PARENT PARTICIPATION

Volunteers are used in classrooms, on field trips and as guest speakers. **Parent education:** None. **Fundraising:** Events include auction, crab feed and festival.

WHAT SETS SCHOOL APART FROM OTHERS?

"Caring parent community, dedicated teachers, lovable students."

HOW DO PARENTS/STUDENTS CHARACTERIZE THE SCHOOL?

"Excellent."

ST. JOSEPH OF CUPERTINO SCHOOL

10120 North DeAnza Blvd.
Cupertino, CA 95014
(408) 252-6441 *fax (408) 252-9771*
www.dsj.org/edu/dsjedu.htm
stjosephup@impresso.com

Mary F. Lyons, *Principal and Admissions*

We are looking for "families who want to forge a strong, supportive working relationship between school and home, for families who want to provide a quality Catholic education for their children." **Our school best serves** "the children of our community."

GENERAL

Co-ed K-8 Catholic parochial school (89% of students are Catholic). Founded 1956. Nonprofit. **Accreditation:** WASC/WCEA. **Enrollment:** 313. **Average class size:** 35. **Length of school year:** 180 days. **Length of school day:** 8:20 a.m.-3 p.m. **Location:** In Cupertino, approximately 10 miles north of San Jose. North De Anza Blvd. is accessible via Interstate 280.

STUDENT BODY

Geographic: Most students come from Cupertino, Sunnyvale, Santa Clara, San Jose and Saratoga. **Ethnicity:** 63.3% Caucasian (non-Latino), 14.7% Asian/Pacific Islander, 12.5% Latino, 5% Filipino, 3.2% Middle Eastern or East Indian, 1.3% African-American. **Foreign students (I-20 status):** .3%. **Two f/t working parent families:** 74.3%. **Single parent families:** 10.4%.

ADMISSION

<u>Kindergarten</u>. **Application deadline:** February. **Age requirement:** 5 years old by December 1. **Application fee:** $25. **Application process:** "Family completes application; child is screened for readiness for grade level. Vacancies are filled according to the following criteria: 1) sibling already attends school; 2) family is active in the parish; 3) child is baptized Catholic." **Preschools visited by admission director:** None. **Number of applications received:** 51 applications received last year for 36 spaces. **Preferences:** See "Application process," above. <u>Other grades</u>. **Application deadline:** February (late applications will be accepted for waiting list). **Application fee:** $25. **Application process:** Same as above; admissions test given. **Test score/GPA cut-off:** N/P. **Estimated number of openings in grades other than K each year:** Nine.

COSTS

Latest tuition: For K, $3,950 for in-parish, $4,500 for out, and $4,950 for non-Catholic; for G1-8, $3,500 for in-parish, $4,050 for out, and $4,950 for non-Catholic. **Last tuition increase:** N/P. **Tuition payment plan:** Available (not specified). **Sibling discount:** Yes, though maximum family tuition cap applies to Catholic families only. **Percentage of students receiving financial aid:** Approximately 10%. **Average grant award:** $1,250. **Number of full tuition grants:** None. **Number of partial tuition grants:** 28; 50% of awards are half-tuition or more.

PROGRAM AND PHILOSOPHY

<u>School's mission statement/goals</u>. "St. Joseph of Cupertino School is committed to educating the 'whole child.' We place equal importance on the spiritual, intellectual, social and physical development of each unique child. We base our education upon the teachings of Jesus—teachings which foster respect, responsibility, justice, gratitude and peacefulness. We believe in forging a strong relationship with the family because we understand that parents are the first and most important teachers of their children. Children benefit when they know that all the adults in their lives are working together and supporting each other. Because we are committed to educating the 'whole child,' our program is very comprehensive. We provide a challenging academic curriculum, while addressing the special needs of individual students. We acknowledge our responsibility to prepare our students for the world in which they will live. We expect them to learn to give back to their world and to believe that they can make it a better place. We

are dedicated to instilling this sense of social responsibility in our students by modeling a praying, learning, growing, caring and welcoming community. We are committed to nurturing the values of the Gospel message in our daily contact with each other, with the students, with the families and with the larger community." **Academic program and philosophy.** "We offer a challenging curriculum. However, we also make every effort to address the special needs of a wide range of students." **Approach to teaching reading:** "Literature-based with a strong phonics foundation; fully correlated with other curricular areas." **Approach to teaching math:** "Emphasis on both concept development and strong computational skills. **Approach to technology and computer training:** All students receive computer training. The school has a computer lab, as well as computers in the classroom. Systems are networked and have Internet access. The school has two specialized computer teachers on its faculty. **Other courses/offerings:** Foreign language is offered after school in grades K-8; also offered are art (K-8), choral music (K-8), instrumental music (K-8, additional fee), and competitive athletics (4-8). **Special programs:** The 6th grade class participates in a full-week science camp experience. **Average nightly homework:** No more than 30 minutes per night for grades 1-2; no more than 45 minutes per night for grade 3; no more than 1 hour per night for grades 4-5; no more than 1.5 hours per night for grade 6; no more than 2 hours per night for grades 7-8. **Grading system for lower school:** "Outstanding," "Successful," "Needs Improvement." **Grading system for middle school:** Letter grades (A-F). **Frequency of parent/teacher conferences:** "Parent-Teacher conferences are required once a year; however, school/home communication is ongoing." **Standardized tests:** N/P. **High schools attended by recent graduates:** St. Francis (14), Mitty (6), Presentation (4), Bellarmine (4), St. Lawrence (4), Cupertino H.S. (public) (1), Lynbrook (public)(1). **Other indicators that the school is accomplishing its goals:** "Our families believe in us and are our greatest public relations spokespersons."

ATHLETICS

Physical education program: Full-time teacher and aide; focus on skill development and fostering a lifelong love of physical activity. The program is fully equipped and has access to a field, track, gym and playground. **Interscholastic athletics:** Students participate in the Girls Parochial Athletic Conference and South Peninsula Catholic Athletic League.

FACULTY

Gender: 100% female. **Ethnicity:** 100% Caucasian (non-Latino). **Highest educational degree held:** Bachelor's 57%, Master's 43%. **Credentials:** All hold California teaching credentials. Two teachers hold special education teaching credentials. **Teacher/student ratio:** 1:36 (lower school), 1:35 (middle school). **Faculty selection and professional development:** "Faculty members are hired by the principal. Credentials are required. The Diocese of San Jose requires ongoing professional development."

Extended Care/After-School Programs

Extended care is offered mornings from 7 a.m. to 8:15 a.m. and from dismissal to 6 p.m. for grades K-8. **Cost:** $2.75/hour for 1st child in family, $1.75 for each additional child. **Drop-in:** Available. **No coverage on:** School holidays. **Snacks:** None provided. **Homework:** Homework time is voluntary. **Staff/child ratio:** Approximately 1:20. **After-school classes:** Spanish, band, art, piano, dance. **Cost:** Approximately $5-$14/week.

Campus Life

Facilities: The campus consists of classrooms, computer lab, science lab, library, art room, religious education center, AV room, parish hall/gymnasium, extended day care center, large play area, grass field with diamond and track, and play structures. **Meals:** Lunch service three times/week (optional). **Transportation:** No school-sponsored transportation. **Uniforms:** Required. **Co-curricular activities/clubs:** Sports, academic decathlon, student council, scouts and yearbook club. **Student support services:** Special education tutor, counseling, advanced math program. **Services for children with learning differences:** Special education teacher. **Counselor/student ratio:** One family counselor (MFCC). **Policies regarding discipline, drug/alcohol use and abuse prevention and AIDS awareness:** "Use of drugs/alcohol constitutes grounds for immediate expulsion. There are curricular programs for drug/alcohol abuse prevention and AIDS awareness." **Summer programs:** Offered at same cost as extended care.

Parent Participation

Parent volunteers are used extensively in a program called Family Service. **Parent education:** Parent education evenings are provided 1-2 times a year. **Fundraising:** Events include auction, magazine sale and scrip. Participation is voluntary.

What Sets School Apart From Others?

"Our [school] philosophy. We truly live by this philosophy in making everyday decisions and in setting policy."

How Do Parents/Students Characterize the School?

"Our parents and students feel as if they 'belong' to a community which supports and nurtures them. They are active, involved, and committed to their school."

ST. JOSEPH'S SCHOOL

50 Emilie Avenue
Atherton, CA 94027
(650) 322-1866
www.shschools.org/sjs

John Miller, *Principal*

Admissions:
150 Valparaiso Avenue
Atherton, CA 94027
(650) 473-4011

Ellen Williamson, *Director of Admission*

GENERAL

Co-ed PreK-8 independent Catholic school. Founded 1906. **Nonprofit**, member, CAIS. **Accreditation:** WASC. **Enrollment**: 395 (K-8). **Average class size:** 24 (with 2 instructors) in grades 1-5, 15-18 in grades 6-8 (50 students per grade). **Length of school year:** N/P. **Length of school day:** N/P. **Location:** Approximately two blocks west of El Camino Real, in Atherton, approximately 25 miles south of San Francisco.

STUDENT BODY

N/P.

ADMISSION

[Ed. Note: The school operates a Preschool and Kindergarten program, known as the St. Joseph's Montessori Preschool and Kindergarten, graduates of which have priority for admission to the primary school program. Preschoolers must be 3 years old by August 31. For preschool information, refer to the SJS web site (www.shschools.org/sjs). A limited number of openings (sometimes 1 or 2) occur in grades 1-5 on a year-to-year basis, with slightly more openings occurring at the 6th grade level when some students depart to attend other middle/high schools.] **Kindergarten. Application deadline:** N/P. **Age requirement:** N/P. **Application fee:** N/P. **Application process:** The application procedure includes a tour (held November-February), application form, teacher recommendations, transcripts/report cards, student statements (middle school) and $40 application fee. Middle School admission testing takes place in January. Following testing, "appropriate" students are invited to shadow for a day and an interview with the parents/student may be requested. Applicants are notified of the final decisions in March. The school seeks "academically capable, socially responsible students."

Preschools visited by admission director: N/P. **Number of applications received:** Ranges from 30 for 1st grade to 60 for 6th grade. **Preferences:** The school will take into account "whether siblings attend St. Joseph's or Sacred Heart Prep; whether either parent is an alumna/us or member of our staff; boy/girl balance." **Other grades.** See above. **Admission test:** N/P. **Test score/GPA cut-off:** N/P. **Estimated number of openings in grades other than K each year:** N/P. **We are looking for:** N/P. **"Our school best serves:** N/P.

COSTS

Latest tuition: $10,500 for PreK-K, $10,900 for grades 1-5, and $12,675 for grades 6-8. Books and fees for grades 1-5 are $100-$250; for grades 6-8, $300-$500. **Latest tuition increase:** N/P. **Tuition payment plans:** N/P. **Financial aid:** "Financial aid is available, and is awarded on the basis of clearly demonstrated need. Financial aid applicants should contact the Admission Office to request the Parent's Financial Statement booklet." **Percentage of students receiving financial aid:** Approximately 10%.

PROGRAM AND PHILOSOPHY

School's mission statement/goals. N/P. (St. Joseph's is a member of the network of Sacred Heart Schools, whose goals include to "educate to a personal and active faith in God, a deep respect for intellectual values, a social awareness which impels to action, the building of community and personal growth in wise freedom.") **Academic philosophy and program.** The lower school curriculum includes courses in foreign languages, fine arts and religion and physical education taught by specialists in addition to core offerings. The middle school "is designed to address the needs of young adolescents with a 'school within a school' environment." All middle school students participate in community service learning projects. **Approach to teaching reading/math/technology and computer training:** N/P. **Average nightly homework:** N/P. **Grading system:** N/P. **Frequency of parent/teacher conferences:** N/P. **Standardized test scores:** N/P. **High schools attended by recent graduates:** 60%-90% of graduates of St. Joseph continue their studies at Sacred Heart Preparatory. Graduates of the latest class also enrolled in Menlo, St. Francis, Philips Andover, Thacher, Bellarmine, Serra, Mercy-Burlingame, Notre Dame, and Convent. **Other indicators that the school is accomplishing its goals:** N/P.

ATHLETICS

Physical education instruction: N/P. **Interscholastic athletics:** Boys in grades 4-8 compete in the South Peninsula Catholic Athletic League, girls compete in the Girls' Parochial Athletic Conference.

Faculty

N/P.

Extended Care Program

Open before school from 7 a.m. to 8:15 a.m., after school from 11:50 a.m. until 6 p.m. **Cost:** Registration fee of $35 plus monthly fee. **Drop-in:** Available for registered students. **No coverage on:** Major holidays. **Snacks:** Provided. **Homework:** Provided by teachers as needed. **Staff/child ratio:** 2:30 (K), 2:35 (grades 1-2). **After-school classes:** Spanish (for additional fee).

Campus Life

Facilities: St. Joseph's shares a large, multi-building campus with Sacred Heart Preparatory. St. Joseph's has its own corner of the campus, including a newly completed multi-purpose building, the Speiker Pavilion. The school has access to facilities on the main campus, including an aquatic center. **Meals:** N/P. **Transportation:** N/P.

Parent Participation

N/P.

What Sets School Apart From Others

N/P.

How Do Parents/Students Characterize School?

N/P.

ST. JUSTIN SCHOOL

2655 Homestead Road
Santa Clara, CA 95051
(408) 248-1094 *fax (408) 246-0691*
www.st-justin.org

Mary Kolbeck, *Principal*

We are looking for "families who are dedicated to Catholic education and participate in their child's education."

GENERAL

Co-ed K-8 Catholic parochial school (98% of students). Founded in 1958. **Nonprofit. Accreditation**: WASC/WCEA. **Enrollment**: 307. **Average class size**: 34. **Length of school year**: 180 days. **Length of school day:** 8:15 a.m.-11:40 a.m. (K), 8:15 a.m.-3 p.m. (grades 1-8). **Location:** In Santa Clara immediately north of San Jose. Accessible via Interstate 280 and the Lawrence Expressway.

STUDENT BODY

Geographic: Most students come from Santa Clara, San Jose, and Cupertino. **Ethnicity:** 72% Caucasian (non-Latino), 13% Latino, 9% Filipino, 4% Asian or Pacific Islander, 2% other. **Foreign students (I-20 status):** None. **Two f/t working parent/single parent families:** N/P.

ADMISSION

Kindergarten. Application deadline: March 1 (call school for exact date). **Age requirement:** 5 years old by December 2. **Application fee:** $35. **Application process:** Developmental screening. **Preschools visited by admission director:** N/P. **Number of applications received:** 35 applications were received last year for 20 spaces. **Preferences:** Siblings, parishioners, children of alumni, non-parishioner Catholics. **Other grades.** Same application deadline and fee. **Admission test:** Testing in mid-March in language arts and math. **Test score/GPA cutoff:** None. **Estimated number of openings in grades other than K each year:** 8. **"Our school best serves ..."** N/P.

COSTS

Latest tuition: For K, $3,026 for in-parish, $3,497 for out, and $3,833 for non-Catholic; for G1-8, $3,497 for in-parish, $3,833 for out, and $3,967 for non-Catholic. **Last tuition increase:** 5% to 6% annually. **Tuition payment plan:** Available. Certain tiers of tuition require use of school scrip and a 36-hour per year commitment to the thrift shop. **Sibling discount:** Substantial. **Percentage of students receiving financial aid:** 15%. **Average grant award:** $1,000.

Number of full tuition grants: One. **Number of partial tuition grants:** 19; 50% for half-tuition or more. **Other information regarding financial assistance:** The Parent Teacher Guild operates a Thrift Store which generates funds for the school's general operating fund.

PROGRAM AND PHILOSOPHY

School's mission statement/goals. "St. Justin, a Catholic elementary school, is dedicated to providing a safe and nurturing environment for all of our students. As partners in the educational process with parents, we strive to be role models as we share the Gospel message and build a community based on peace and justice. We offer an excellent educational program which addresses the needs of the whole child while challenging and encouraging students to grow spiritually, academically, socially and physically." **Academic program. Approach to teaching reading/math:** N/P. **Approach to technology and computer training:** Computer lab with 36 computers, four computers in each classroom on school-wide network. Keyboarding begins in 1st grade using "Type to Learn." The school has three computer teachers (one for grades 1-3, one for grades 4-5 and one for grades 6-8) and a technology coordinator. **Other courses/offerings:** Spanish (certain grades only), music (choral and instrumental), athletics. **Special programs:** Science camp in 6th grade. Choir for grades 1-8. **Average nightly homework:** 60 minutes. **Grading system for lower school:** In Kindergarten: "Introduced," "Demonstrates Skill Regularly," "Needs Improvement." Grades 1-3: "Outstanding," "Successful," "Needs Improvement." **Grading system for middle school:** Letter grades (A-F). **Frequency of parent/teacher conferences:** Once a year and as needed or requested. General parent communication also takes place through newsletters. **Standardized test scores:** Provided to parents only (child's scores). **High schools attended by recent graduates:** Santa Clara High School, Prospect, Cupertino, St. Francis, Bellarmine, Mitty, Lincoln, St. Lawrence. **Other indicators that the school is accomplishing its goals:** "Positive feedback from high schools."

ATHLETICS

Physical education program: P.E. is offered two days per week for 30 minutes; units include volleyball, basketball, dance, etc. **Interscholastic athletics:** "The St. Justin School Athletic Program is open to all students in grades 5-8. It is a developmental program and students learn from the beginning how to play team sports. The focus of our program is to teach good team skills and allow students to improve and play. All students who sign up to play are on the team. Attendance at practice is required for continuation on the team. We are proud to offer flag football, volleyball, basketball, and softball."

FACULTY

Gender: 85% female, 15% male. **Ethnicity:** 90% Caucasian (non-Latino), 10% Latino. **Highest educational degree held:** Bachelor's 100%. **Credentials:** Nine teachers have California teaching credentials. **Teacher/student ratio:** 2:30 (K), 2:35 (grades 1-2), and 1:35 (grades 3-8). **Faculty training and professional development:** Applications are reviewed by the personnel department of the San Jose Diocese; candidates are interviewed. Teaching credentials are required. Teachers participate in in-service programs throughout the year.

EXTENDED CARE/AFTER-SCHOOL PROGRAMS

Open before school from 7 a.m. to 8:15 a.m., after school from 11:50 a.m. until 6 p.m. **Cost:** Registration fee of $35 plus monthly fee. **Drop-in:** Available for registered students. **No coverage on:** Major holidays. **Snacks:** Provided. **Homework:** Provided by teachers as needed. **Staff/child ratio:** 2:30 (K), 2:35 (grades 1-2). **After-school classes:** Spanish (for additional fee).

CAMPUS LIFE

Facilities: The school building consists of three wings, 17 classrooms, and a large and a small hall. Students use class libraries and the city library next door to the school. **Meals:** Lunch service is available daily. **Transportation:** No school-sponsored transportation. **Uniforms:** Required. **Co-curricular activities/clubs:** Student council. **Student support services:** N/P. **Services for children with learning differences:** Learning specialist on staff. **Counselor/student ratio:** 1:307. **Policies regarding discipline, drug/alcohol use and abuse prevention and AIDS awareness:** "Discipline is considered an aspect of moral guidance; rules are set. Students participate in D.A.R.E. program; AIDS lessons taught." **Summer programs:** Six-week program designed to maintain skills students have mastered. Concentration of language and math. In addition, students have art, science, computers, field trips, speakers, and P.E.

PARENT PARTICIPATION

Family Service commitment of 36 hours in the on-site thrift shop. Parents may also volunteer in the "PTG" (Parent-Teacher Guild) program. **Parent education:** Offered through Center for Family Development. **Fundraising:** Events include "Robin Wrap," "Jog-a-thon," and "Monte Carlo."

WHAT SETS SCHOOL APART FROM OTHERS?

N/P.

HOW DO PARENTS/STUDENTS CHARACTERIZE THE SCHOOL?

"A school that provides a good education, Catholic values and instruction, feeling or belonging to a community, and a caring, competent staff."

ST. LAWRENCE ELEMENTARY AND MIDDLE SCHOOLS

1977 Lawrence Drive
Santa Clara, CA 95951
(408) 296-2260 *fax (408) 296-1068*
www.saintlawrence.org
slems@stlawrence.org

Priscilla Murphy, *Principal*
Arlene Cimino, *Assistant Principal* (admissions)

GENERAL

Co-ed PreK-8 Catholic parochial school (80% of students are Catholic). Founded in 1961. **Nonprofit. Accreditation:** WASC/WCEA (through 2004). **Enrollment:** 450. **Average class size:** 35. **Length of school year:** 180 days. **Length of school day:** 8 a.m.-3 p.m. **Location:** Off Lawrence Expressway.

STUDENT BODY

Geographic: Most students come from Santa Clara, Sunnyvale, San Jose, Cupertino, Milpitas, Gilroy, San Mateo, and Fremont. **Ethnicity:** 33% Caucasian (non-Latino), 32% Asian/Pacific Islander, 21% Filipino, 14% Latino, .03% Middle Eastern or East Indian, .03% African-American, .01% Native American. **Foreign students:** None. **Two f/t working parent families:** 85%. **Single parent families:** 7%.

ADMISSION

<u>Kindergarten</u>. **Application deadline:** Open. **Age requirement:** 5 years old by December 1. **Application fee:** $40. **Application process:** Readiness screening. **Preschools visited by admissions director:** None. **Number of applications received:** 35 applications received last year for 70 spaces; 20 spaces filled by school's own preschool students. **Preferences:** Siblings, Catholics. <u>Other grades</u>. **Application deadline:** Open. **Application fee:** $40. **Application process:** Standardized Achievement Test. **Test score/GPA cut-off:** N/P. **Estimated number of openings in grades other than K:** Grades 1-5, 2 each; grades 6, 25-30; grades 7 and 8, 2 each. **"We are looking for "** N/P. **"Our school best serves"** N/P.

COSTS

Latest tuition: $4,525 for K-5, $4,620 for grades 6-8. (Qualifying Catholic students are eligible for a 20% discount.) **Tuition payment plan:** Available. **Sibling discount:** Substantial. **Percentage of students receiving financial aid:**

11%. **Average grant award, number of full tuition grants and number of partial tuition grants:** N/P. **Other:** Must be enrolled in the school for at least one year to apply for financial aid.

PROGRAM AND PHILOSOPHY

School's mission statement/goals. "St. Lawrence is a Catholic elementary and middle school which promotes the growth of the whole child and provides a solid spiritual formation and academic foundation for living in the third millennium." **Academic program. Approach to teaching reading:** N/P. **Approach to teaching math:** N/P. **Approach to technology and computer training:** Computer lab and classroom computers. "Computer education is incorporated into the curriculum by the classroom teacher. Keyboarding instruction at appropriate grade levels." The school has a computer specialist on faculty. Campus computers are networked. Internet access. Students have access to computers at lunchtime. **Other courses/offerings** Religion is taught daily; Family Life Program, regular prayer services and all-school Liturgies; all day Kindergarten; staggered reading program in grades K-2; standardized testing for grades 2-8 in September; textbooks updated as set forth by the Diocese of San Jose; music taught twice weekly by a specialist in music education; Japanese in grades 1-5, Spanish in grades 6-8; choral music. **Special programs:** Regular field trips, including 6th grade science camp and retreats for grades 6-8. Annual Fine Arts Fair/Science Fair. **Average nightly homework:** N/P. **Grading system for lower school:** "O, S, N." **Grading system for middle school (grades 4-8):** "A, B, C, D, F." **Frequency of parent/teacher conferences:** One conference at the end of the 1st quarter, weekly newsletter. **High schools attended by recent graduates:** 95% go on to Diocesan and private Catholic high schools, including Bellarmine, Mitty, St. Francis, Presentation, Notre Dame and St. Lawrence Academy. **Other indicators that the school is accomplishing its goals:** "Full 6-year WASC accreditation term."

ATHLETICS

Physical education program: P.E. classes are taught by a specialist; K-2 motor perception program. The school facilities include a swimming pool. **Interscholastic athletics:** The school competes in the West Valley Athletic League. Girls in grades 5-8 compete in volleyball, basketball and softball; boys in grades 5-8 compete in flag football, basketball and volleyball. Parish swim team.

FACULTY

Gender: 75% female, 25% male. **Ethnicity:** 99% Caucasian (non-Latino), 1% Latino. **Teacher/student ratio:** 17-18:1 in lower school, 34:1 in upper school. **Highest educational degree held:** Bachelor's 75%, Masters 25%. **California teaching credential:** 50%. **Faculty selection and professional development:** Selected by "interview and qualifications." Teachers participate in "mandatory professional growth each year."

Extended Care/After-School Program

Extended care is offered mornings from 6:45 a.m. and until 6 p.m. in the evening for grades K-8. (Pre-K extended care begins at 7 a.m.) **Cost:** $3.80/hour. **Drop-in:** Available. **No coverage on:** Good Friday, Thanksgiving, Christmas and New Year's Day. **Snacks:** Provided. **Homework:** Homework is mandatory; assistance is provided. **Staff/child ratio:** 1:5 in K-8 (1:12 in Pre-K program). **Other:** The school runs camps during Christmas, winter and Easter breaks.

Campus Life

Facilities: Campus facilities include a library, computer lab, gymnasium/auditorium, swimming pool, educational television and VCR in each classroom, and science lab. **Meals:** Hot lunch program daily. **Transportation:** No school-sponsored transportation. **Uniforms:** Required. **Co-curricular activities/clubs:** Activities include parish-sponsored Boy/Girl Scouts. **Student support services:** N/P. **Services for students with learning differences:** Outreach tutorial program (additional fee). **Counselor/student ratio:** N/P. **Policies regarding discipline, drug/alcohol use and abuse prevention and AIDS awareness:** N/P. **Summer programs:** Camp for grades entering K through 5 featuring arts and crafts, swimming, group sports, games, and activities. Weekly fee (approximately $125).

Parent Participation

Each family must volunteer 20 hours per year. **Parent education:** N/P. **Fundraising:** Events include candy drive, magazine drive, walk-a-thon. Mandatory participation in one event yearly.

What Sets School Apart From Others?

"Multi-cultural student body and caring environment."

How Do Parents/Students Characterize the School?

"Caring, challenging—a great place to learn."

ST. LUCY SCHOOL

76 Kennedy Avenue
Campbell, CA 95008
(408) 871-8023 *fax (408) 378-4945*
www.stlucyschool.org
stlucy@aol.com

Sister Jolene M. Schmitz, *Principal and Admissions Director*

GENERAL

Co-ed K-8 Catholic parochial school (97% of students are Catholic). Founded in 1953. **Nonprofit. Accreditation:** WASC (through 2002). **Enrollment:** 318. **Average class size:** 35. **Length of school year:** 180 days. **Length of school day:** 8:13 a.m.-3 p.m. **Location:** In Campbell, west of and adjacent to San Jose. Nearest cross street is S. Winchester Blvd.

STUDENT BODY

Geographic: Most students come from Campbell and San Jose. **Ethnicity:** 80% Caucasian (non-Latino), 13% Latino, 4% Filipino, 2% Asian/Pacific Islander, 1% African-American. **Foreign students (I-20 status):** None. **Two f/t working parent families:** 75%. **Single parent families:** 15%.

ADMISSION

Kindergarten. Application deadline: February 2 (check with school for exact date for current year). **Age requirement:** 5 years old by December 1 of Kindergarten year. **Application fee:** $25. **Application process:** The school administers the Brigance test. **Preschools visited by the admission director:** N/P. **Number of applications received:** 55 applications were received last year for 36 spaces. **Preferences:** Siblings and parish members. **Other grades. Application deadline:** February 19 (check with school for exact date for current year). **Application fee:** $25. **Application process/testing:** Teacher-made test and visit to class by prospective student. **Test score/GPA cut-off:** None. **Estimated number of openings in grades other than K each year:** Three. **"We are looking for ..."** N/P. **"Our school best serves ..."** N/P.

COSTS

Latest tuition: Approximately $2,800-$3,200 for one child. The school has three tuition categories: In-parish status, participatory (active in another parish), and non-participatory. **Last tuition increase:** N/P. **Tuition payment plan:** Available (e.g., 10-month plan). **Sibling discount:** Substantial. **Percentage of students receiving financial aid:** 17%. **Average grant award:** $600. **Number of full**

tuition grants: None. **Number of partial tuition grants:** Five, three of which were half-tuition or more. **Other information regarding financial assistance:** St. Lucy Parish and the Diocese of San Jose both have scholarship funds. Applications are made each spring.

PROGRAM AND PHILOSOPHY

School's mission statement/goals. "St. Lucy School is a total educational environment committed to maximizing each child's potential and advancing the spiritual, intellectual, physical, psychological and social needs [of its students]. St. Lucy School is a Catholic community, teaching the gospel message wherein the value of students, parents, staff and community are recognized and developed." Academic program. **Approach to teaching reading:** N/P. **Approach to teaching math:** N/P. **Approach to technology and computer training:** N/P. **Other courses/offerings:** Foreign languages are offered in grades 5-8 (language not specified), choral music in grades K-5, instrumental music (for additional fee), and after-school athletics for grades 5-8. **Special programs:** Outdoor education for grade 6. **Average nightly homework:** 10-20 minutes (K-2), 30-60 minutes (grades 3-5), 60-90 minutes (grades 6-8). **Grading system for lower school (K-3):** "Outstanding, Satisfactory, Unsatisfactory." **Grading system for upper school (4-8):** Letter grades (A-F). **Frequency of parent/teacher conferences:** Once a year is mandatory, other conferences as needed. **Standardized test scores:** N/P. **High schools attended by recent graduates:** Mitty (16), Bellarmine (8), St. Lawrence (4), Presentation (4), Notre Dame (2), public high school (2). **Other indicators that the school is achieving its goals:** N/P.

ATHLETICS

Physical education program: N/P. **Interscholastic athletics:** The school competes in the West Valley Athletic League in basketball, volleyball, flag football (boys), softball (girls), and track.

FACULTY

Gender: 90% female, 10% male. **Ethnicity:** 91% Caucasian (non-Latino), 6% Latino, 3% African-American. **Highest educational degree held:** 80% Bachelor's, 20% Master's. **Credentials:** Ten teachers have California teaching credentials, three have other credentials and/or training. **Teacher/student ratio:** 1:35. **Faculty selection and professional development:** Teachers are hired through the Diocese of San Jose Personnel Office.

EXTENDED CARE/AFTER-SCHOOL PROGRAMS

Extended care is offered from 6:45 a.m. until school begins and after school until 6 p.m. **Cost:** $2.50/hour. **Drop-in:** Available. **No coverage on:** School holidays. **Snacks:** Provided. **Homework:** Homework time is voluntary, assistance is provided. **Staff/child ratio:** 1:15. **After-school classes:** None.

CAMPUS LIFE

Facilities: The campus consists of three buildings, nine classrooms, computer lab, library, reading room, resource center, gym, large meeting room and separate extended care building. **Meals:** Hot lunch on Tuesday only. **Transportation:** No school-sponsored transportation. **Uniforms:** Required. **Co-curricular activities/clubs:** N/P. **Student support services:** N/P. **Services for children with learning differences:** N/P. **Counselor/student ratio:** N/P. **Policies regarding discipline, drug/alcohol use and abuse prevention and AIDS awareness:** N/P. **Summer programs:** Offered for $250 for 4-week program.

PARENT PARTICIPATION

40 hours for 2-parent families, 20 hours for single-parent families. **Parent education:** N/P. **Fundraising:** Parents work ten hours over a three day weekend event.

WHAT SETS SCHOOL APART FROM OTHERS?

N/P.

HOW DO PARENTS/STUDENTS CHARACTERIZE THE SCHOOL?

N/P.

ST. MARTIN SCHOOL

597 Central Avenue
Sunnyvale, CA 94086
(408) 736-5534 *fax (408) 736-1043*

Rosemary Griggs, *Principal and Admissions,* rgriggs@stmartinsun.org

Our school best serves "students without major learning differences - no special ed. teacher available."

GENERAL

Co-ed PreK-8 Catholic parochial school (75% of students). Founded: N/P. **Nonprofit. Accreditation:** WCEA/WASC (6-year term). **Enrollment:** 345. **Average class size:** 35. **Length of school year:** Approximately 181 days. **Length of school day:** Grades 1-8, 8:15 a.m. to 3 p.m. Kindergarten sessions run from 8:15 a.m. to 11:30 a.m. and 11:45 a.m. to 3 p.m. PreK hours are 8:15 a.m. to 11:15 a.m. **Location:** In Sunnyvale, approximately 10 miles north of downtown

San Jose. Nearest cross street is Old San Francisco Road; school is accessible via the Central Expressway or El Camino.

STUDENT BODY

Geographic: Most students come from Sunnyvale. **Ethnicity:** N/P. **Foreign students:** None. **Two f/t working parent families:** 80%. **Single parent families:** 5%.

ADMISSION

<u>Kindergarten</u>. **Application deadline:** Ongoing. **Age requirement:** 5 years old by December 2. **Application fee:** $25. **Application process:** Testing, review of past records, interview. **Preschools visited by admission director:** N/P. **Number of applications received:** The school received 53 applications last year for 14 spaces ("varies from year to year"). Students from the PreK program filled the remaining 22 spaces. **Preferences:** Siblings, parishioners. <u>**Other grades.**</u> Same as above, except that applicants are also tested. (N/P re test) **Test score/GPA cutoff:** N/P. **Estimated number of openings in grades other than K each year:** 10. **"We are looking for ..."** N/P.

COSTS

Latest tuition: In parish: $2,728 for K, $3,157 for one child in G1-8, $5,522 for 2, $6,776 for 3. Out-of-parish: $3,267 for K, $3,784 for one child in G1-8, $6,622 for 2, $8,140 for 3. **Latest tuition increase:** N/P. **Tuition payment plan:** Available. **Sibling discount:** See above. **Percentage of students receiving financial aid:** N/P. **Average grant award:** N/P. **Number of full tuition grants**: None. **Number of partial tuition grants:** 15, none of half-tuition or more.

PROGRAM AND PHILOSOPHY

<u>School's philosophy.</u> "As Christian educators, we first strive to provide and nurture an environment in which the teachings of Jesus Christ can be learned and lived. Secondly, we seek to create an atmosphere of learning that will encourage the growth of knowledgeable and creative individuals with a desire for life-long learning. In partnership with family and church, St. Martin School is a community of faith. Students will develop a foundation of Catholic values and learn to contribute positively to church, parish and society as witnessed by leadership and service. We believe that education is a cooperative venture of exploration, interaction, and discovery of self, others and the world. This takes place most effectively in an atmosphere that fosters the spiritual, intellectual, psychological, social and physical potentials of each member. We strive to share this vision motivated by the teachings of Jesus and by the message of the Gospel." **Academic program.** "A structured [program with] high academic standards." **Approach to teaching reading/math:** N/P. **Approach to technology and computer training:** The school has a computer lab with 38 computers, as well as six computers

in each classroom. All computers are networked. The computer is "used as a tool." Internet access is available. **Other courses/offerings:** Spanish (after-school class), choral music for grades 1-8, instrumental music for grades 4-8, and athletics. **Special programs:** 6th grade science camp, 2nd grade sacramental program. **Average nightly homework:** 15 minutes to 1.75 hours, depending upon grade. **Grading system for grades 1-3:** O ("Outstanding Achievement"), S ("Successful Achievement") and N ("Needs Improvement"). **Grading system for grades 4-8:** Letter grades (A-F). (Report cards for all grade levels include a section for comments to elaborate on grade/assessment.) **Frequency of parent/teacher conferences:** All parent conferences are held at the end of 1st quarter and on-going as needed. **Standardized test scores:** Provided to parents (child's own scores) only. **High schools attended by recent graduates:** St. Francis, Mitty, St. Lawrence and Fremont (public). (Most students go on to Catholic schools.) **Other indicators that the school is accomplishing its goals:** N/P.

ATHLETICS

Physical education program: Once a week students receive instruction from a certified P.E. instructor. **Interscholastic athletics:** Grades 4-8 participate in the after-school leagues (SPCAL for boys and GPAC for girls).

FACULTY

Gender: "All but one instructor is female." **Ethnicity:** 100% Caucasian (non-Latino). **Highest educational degree held:** Five have Master's degrees, three are close to completing their Master's degrees. **Credentials:** All teachers are credentialed. **Teacher/student ratio:** 1:35. **Faculty training and professional development:** The school requires all teachers to have teaching credentials, provides in-service training, and encourages continuing education.

EXTENDED CARE/AFTER-SCHOOL PROGRAMS

Extended care is available from 6 a.m. to 6 p.m. **Cost:** $3/hour or $12 maximum; $2/hour for 2nd child and $1/hour for additional children from same family. **Drop-in:** Available. **No coverage on:** School holidays except for local and Diocesan in-service days. **Snacks:** N/P. **Homework:** Homework time is mandatory and is supervised by teachers. **Staff/student ratio:** N/P. **After-school classes:** Spanish is offered for additional fee.

CAMPUS LIFE

Facilities: N/P. The campus includes a library. **Meals:** Lunch/meal service is available. **Transportation:** No school-sponsored transportation. **Uniforms:** Required. **Co-curricular activities/clubs:** N/P. **Student support services:** N/P. **Services for children with learning differences:** None. **Counselor/student ratio:** N/P. **Policies regarding discipline, drug/alcohol use and abuse prevention and**

AIDS awareness: "We have a parent/student handbook." **Summer programs:** Six-week program of morning academics and afternoon sports, games and crafts.

PARENT PARTICIPATION

No minimum number of hours. Volunteers may work as "classroom aides, field trip drivers, in the office, on fundraising, etc." **Parent education:** "Ongoing." **Fundraising:** Events include candy sale and magazine sales.

WHAT SETS SCHOOL APART FROM OTHERS?

"High academic standards, drug-free, gang-free, caring, committed teachers and a positive atmosphere."

HOW DO PARENTS/STUDENTS CHARACTERIZE THE SCHOOL?

"A caring community and devoted staff."

ST. MARTIN OF TOURS ELEMENTARY SCHOOL

300 O'Conner Drive
San Jose, CA 95128
(408) 287-3630 *fax (408) 287-4313*
www.stmartin.org
stmartin@aol.com

Mrs. Karen DeMonner, *Principal*

We are looking for "parish children who after screening are ready for our Kindergarten program." **Our school best serves** "parish children of average or above average intelligence."

GENERAL

Co-ed K-8 Catholic parochial school (98.9% of students are Catholic). Founded 1955. **Nonprofit. Accreditation**: WASC/WCEA. **Enrollment**: 352. **Average class size**: 35. **Length of school year**: 180 days. **Length of school day:** 8 a.m.-2:50 p.m. **Location:** In San Jose in the vicinity of Valley Fair Shopping Center and O'Conner Hospital. Accessible via Interstate 280.

Student Body

Geographic: Most students come from San Jose and Santa Clara. **Ethnicity:** 79% Caucasian (non-Latino), 9% Latino, 5% Asian/Pacific Islander, 4% Filipino, 2% African-American, 1% other. **Foreign students:** None. **Two f/t working parent families:** 85%. **Single parent families:** 5%.

Admission

<u>Kindergarten</u>. **Application deadline:** Mid-February (check with school for exact date). **Age requirement:** 4 years, 9 months (as of beginning of school year). **Application fee:** $40 (includes screening). **Application process:** "Each applicant is screened for readiness for our K program." **Preschools visited by admission director:** N/P. **Number of applications received:** 67 applications were received last year for 36 spaces. **Preferences:** Siblings, parishioners. <u>Other grades</u>. **Application deadline:** Mid-February (check with school for exact date.) **Application fee:** $20. **Application process:** "If we have any openings, the child is screened for readiness for that grade." **Admission test:** Given in mid-March. (N/P re test) **Test score/GPA cut-off:** N/P. **Estimated number of openings in grades other than K each year:** "One or two."

Costs

Latest tuition: $3,776 for one parish child, $6,390 for two, and $8,850 for three. For out-of-parish, $4,307 per child. **Latest tuition increase:** N/P. **Tuition payment plan:** Available (monthly or 10-month). **Sibling discount:** 35% of tuition. **Percentage of students receiving financial aid:** 5%. **Average grant award:** $750. **Number of full tuition grants**: None. **Number of partial tuition grants:** 15, all for less than half-tuition. **Other information regarding financial assistance:** "Must be an active parish member."

Program and Philosophy

<u>School's mission statement/goals</u>. "St. Martin of Tours Elementary School is a parish school rich in the tradition of Catholic education and committed to academic excellence. Together with the family and parish community, we are dedicated to creating an enthusiastic vision of the future. Together, we teach the message of the gospels and formation of Christian values. Together, we value the uniqueness and dignity of each person and promote a warm and welcoming community. Together, we challenge our students and ourselves to develop the skills to think critically, to express ourselves creatively and to act responsibly as we become true agents of the gospel." **Academic program. Approach to teaching reading/math:** Follow Diocesan guidelines. **Approach to technology and computer training:** "Over 50 Apple Computers, networked. Time is given during the school week for computer training." **Other courses/offerings:** French in lower grades, Spanish in grades 7-8, art, drama, choral music, instrumental music (grades 4-8, for additional fee), and after-school athletics for grades 5-8. **Special**

programs: Eighth grade musical in the spring, 8th grade trip to Yosemite for 5 days, 6th grade trip to Marin Headlands, 5th grade Maritime overnight in San Francisco, and 4th grade overnight trip to the gold country. **Average nightly homework:** Nothing is usually assigned for K; not to exceed 30 minutes on average for grades 1-2; not to exceed 1 hour on average for grades 3-4; not to exceed 1.5 hours on average for grades 5-6; not to exceed 2.5 hours on average for grades 7-8. **Grading system for lower school:** O ("Outstanding"), S ("Satisfactory") and N ("Needs Improvement"). **Grading system for upper school (4-8):** Letter grades (A-F). Report cards issued four times a year. The School uses the Diocese of San Jose report card form. The form has space for comments to elaborate on specific grades and assessments. **Frequency of parent/teacher conferences:** Every parent is scheduled for one fall conference and can request a spring conference. **Standardized test scores:** Provided to parents (child's own scores) and school community (school's overall performance.) **High schools attended by recent graduates:** Mitty (29), Bellarmine (12), Presentation (12), St. Francis (5), Notre Dame (2) and public schools (9). **Other indicators the school is accomplishing its goals:** "Filled to capacity with large waiting lists."

ATHLETICS

Physical education program: Daily classes for grades 1-8. **Interscholastic athletics:** Part of the West Valley Youth League for grades 5-8. Girls play softball, volleyball, and basketball and boys play football, volleyball and basketball.

FACULTY

Gender: 85% female, 15% male. (The school employs more than 30 teachers and staff.) **Ethnicity:** 90% Caucasian (non-Latino), 10% Latino. **Highest educational degree held:** 80% Bachelor's, 20% Master's. **Credentials:** 20% of teachers have California teaching credentials. **Teacher/student ratio:** 1:12. **Faculty selection and professional development:** Faculty positions are filled through application to the Diocese of San Jose.

EXTENDED CARE/AFTER-SCHOOL PROGRAMS

Extended care is available for all grades, from 7 a.m. to 6 p.m. **Cost:** $3.25/hour per student. **Drop-in:** Available. **No coverage on:** School holidays. **Snacks:** Provided. **Homework:** Homework time is mandatory at request of parents. Caregivers provide assistance. **Staff/child ratio:** 1:12. **After-school classes:** None.

CAMPUS LIFE

Facilities: The campus consists of two buildings, a gym and grass field. The school has its own library. **Meals:** Hot lunch is provided twice a week. **Transportation:** No school-sponsored transportation. **Uniforms:** Required. **Co-curricular activities/clubs:** Include student council and pep club, community outreach and service, student-planned liturgies, televised student news, and drama productions. **Student support services:** Counseling (one counselor to 352 students). **Services for students with learning differences:** Tutor and learning assistance program. **Policies regarding discipline, drug/alcohol use and abuse prevention and AIDS awareness:** "Education through grade levels. D.A.R.E." **Summer programs:** None.

PARENT PARTICIPATION

No minimum hours required of parents. The school uses volunteers to run all school events, including tournaments. **Parent education:** Educational evenings provided by the Parent Guild by grade. **Fundraising:** Candy sales, auction, scrip.

WHAT SETS SCHOOL APART FROM OTHERS?

"Location, reputation [and] many programs provided."

HOW DO PARENTS/STUDENTS CHARACTERIZE THE SCHOOL?

"Parents are very involved and willing to help in any way. Students are academically and socially prepared for high school. The school has a very low attrition rate."

ST. MATTHEW'S EPISCOPAL DAY SCHOOL

16 Baldwin Avenue
San Mateo, CA 94401
(650) 342-5436 *fax (650) 342-4019*
www.stmatthewsonline.org

Mark C. Hale, *Head of School*
Linda A. Handalian, *Admission Coordinator*

We are looking for "students who will be successful in a setting that offers a rigorous academic program and a strong foundation of values." **Our school best serves** "students and families that recognize the importance of educating the whole child and each person's role in this process."

GENERAL

Co-ed PreK-8th grade day school. Episcopal (15% of students are Episcopalian). Founded 1953. **Nonprofit**, member CAIS/NAIS. **Accreditation:** CAIS. **Enrollment**: 228. **Average class size:** 22. **Length of school year:** 180 days. **Length of school day:** 8:10 a.m.-3 p.m. (lower school), 8:10 a.m.-3:30 p.m. (middle school). **Location:** In San Mateo, approximately 18 miles south of San Francisco. The school is located near El Camino Real, at the edge of San Mateo's business district, near Mills Peninsula Hospital.

STUDENT BODY

Geographic: Most students come from San Mateo, Foster City, Hillsborough, Burlingame, San Carlos, Redwood City, and Half Moon Bay. **Ethnicity:** 78% Caucasian (non-Latino), 17.5% Asian/Pacific Islander, 2% Middle Eastern or East Indian, 2.5% Latino. **Foreign students (I-20 status):** N/P. **Two f/t working/single parent families:** N/P.

ADMISSION

<u>Kindergarten.</u> **Application deadline:** N/P. (Note that the application can be downloaded from the school's website.) **Age requirement:** 5 years old by September 1. **Application fee:** $75. **Application process:** N/P. **Preschools visited by admission director:** N/P. **Number of applications received:** 26 applications were received last year for 5 spaces; the other 15 spaces in the incoming K class were filled from the preschool. **Preferences:** Siblings, parishioners of St. Matthew's. <u>Other grades.</u> **Application deadline:** Late February. **Application fee:** $75. **Application process:** Grades 1-5: In-house academic testing. Grades 6-8: ISEE Testing from the Educational Records Bureau. **Test score/GPA cut-off:** None. **Estimated number of openings in grades other than K each year:** "Unable to predict; related to re-enrollment which was 91% for last academic year."

COSTS

Latest tuition: $6,500 (3-year-old preschool), $8,000 (4-year-old preschool), $10,900 (K-4), and $12,000 (grades 5-8). Includes fees. **Latest tuition increase:** Approximately 7%. **Tuition payment plan:** Monthly, semi-annual, and annual payment plans are available. (Tuition insurance is required for monthly and bi-annual plans.) **Sibling discount:** None. **Percentage of students receiving financial aid:** 7%. **Average grant award:** $3,500. **Number of full tuition grants:** None. **Number of partial tuition grants:** 18%. **Percentage of all grants that are half-tuition or more:** N/P.

PROGRAM AND PHILOSOPHY

<u>School's mission statement/goals.</u> "The mission of St. Matthew's Episcopal Day School is to provide a solid foundation for lifelong learning, to instill a sense of social responsibility and to reinforce a commitment to excellence through an academically challenging course of study permeated with Christian principles. The core values that help to define our school as Episcopal can best be summarized in the following statement of beliefs. We believe that: We are all one, integrated as a global family. The school will provide an atmosphere guided by the Episcopal tradition in such a way that there is an appreciation for the diversity

and values of all faith traditions. The school will provide age appropriate, engaging opportunities for worship and the development of spiritual life. Our goal is to nurture the spirituality of each member of our community, not to convert. All people are to be treated with equality and dignity for who they are and who they can become. All people are essentially good, and love, compassion, unselfishness and each person's search for truth have greater power than hate, enmity and self-interest. A spirit of free inquiry, unfettered by dogma, should pervade our academic and spiritual programs. Each member of our school community should feel free to appropriately engage in ethical and religious discussion. Each member of our school community should grow in service to others." **Academic program.** **Approach to teaching reading:** Phonics and literature. **Approach to teaching math:** Exploration of numbers, patterns and shapes in K, moving into basic skill building. **Approach to technology and computer training:** N/P. (The school has a technology coordinator and computer lab with carts of computers to take to classrooms.) **Other courses/offerings:** French (PreK-8th grade), music (choral, grades 2-8), instrumental music (private lessons available), art, religion, technology and computer instruction, and physical education. (Middle school students have homeroom and change classrooms for each subject.) **Special programs:** Fourth grade overnight trip to gold country, 5th grade trip to gold country and Sacramento, 6th grade outdoor education, 7th grade 3-day retreat and Yosemite trip, 8th grade 3-day retreat and Washington, D.C. trip. Community service. **Average nightly homework:** 20 minutes for grades 1-2, 30-45 minutes for grade 3, 30-45 minutes for grade 4 during 1st and 2nd trimesters and 60-90 minutes for 3rd trimester, 60-120 minutes for grade 5-6, 120-150 minutes for grade 7-8. **Grading system:** "The School uses several methods for evaluating and reporting academic progress." The academic year is divided into trimesters. At the end of each term parents receive a report card summarizing child's progress. **Frequency of parent/teacher conferences:** Parent/teacher conferences are regularly scheduled for all families. In addition, parents are encouraged to arrange conferences with teachers or administrators whenever there is a special reason to discuss a student's work or progress." **Standardized test scores:** Provided to parents (child's own scores). **High schools attended by recent graduates:** Graduates attend a number of private and public high schools, including Crystal Springs, Menlo, and Sacred Heart. **Other indicators that the school is accomplishing its goals:** "Strong parental support for fundraising program."

ATHLETICS

Physical education program: Part of curriculum. **Interscholastic athletics:** An athletic director coordinates and supervises the after-school program for G5-8.

FACULTY

Gender: 75% female, 25% male. **Ethnicity:** 79% Caucasian, 9% Asian/Pacific Islander, 6% African-American, 3% Native American, 3% Middle Eastern or East Indian. **Highest educational degree held:** Several hold advanced degrees.

Credentials: Several hold California teaching credentials and/or other credentials or training. **Teacher/student ratio:** N/P. **Faculty training and professional development:** N/P.

EXTENDED CARE/AFTER-SCHOOL PROGRAMS

Extended care is available for an additional fee from 7:15 a.m. to 8 a.m. and from 3 p.m. to 3:30 p.m. (sibling/carpool wait) and from 2:30 p.m. to 6 p.m. After-school extended care is usually offered on minimum days. **Cost:** $200 and $265 per month. **Drop-in:** N/P. **No coverage on:** N/P. **Snacks:** Provided. **Homework:** N/P. **Staff/student ratio:** N/P. **After-school classes:** N/P.

CAMPUS LIFE

Facilities: The campus consists of a cluster of buildings around the St. Matthew's Episcopal Church in San Mateo. It includes a classroom and administrative building with a library, two paved outdoor play areas, a lawn area, and a hall for lunch and theater. **Meals:** Hot lunches may be ordered in advance on Thursdays. **Transportation:** No school-sponsored transportation. **Uniforms:** Required for 1st-8th graders. **Co-curricular activities/clubs:** Student council, community service, school newsletter. **Student support services:** "None on campus; outside referrals are made." **Services for children with learning differences:** None. **Counselor/student ratio:** N/A. **Policies regarding discipline, drug/alcohol use and abuse prevention and AIDS awareness:** "Described in handbook in detail." **Summer programs:** None.

PARENT PARTICIPATION

"Extensive use of volunteers. 40 hours per year are required for families in grades 1-8; 20 hours per year for preschool, K, and single parent families. Most families volunteer above minimum." **Parent education:** N/P. (The school distributes newsletters with parenting information.) **Fundraising:** Events include the Annual Appeal (no minimum contribution, but families are expected to participate), Dickens House (time commitment) and auction (participation is voluntary). Other: Mandatory chapel service every morning. Parents are welcome to attend.

WHAT SETS SCHOOL APART FROM OTHERS?

N/P.

HOW DO PARENTS/STUDENTS CHARACTERIZE THE SCHOOL?

"St. Matthew's embodies strong values, solid academics, and a warm sense of community."

ST. VICTOR SCHOOL

3150 Sierra Road
San Jose, CA 95123
(408) 251-1740 *fax (408) 251-1492*
www.stvictor.org

Sister Sharon Breden, *Principal*, sbreden@stvictor.org

We are looking for "a family whose child is ready for our program academically and will support the school and child." **Our school best serves** "the average child from a value-oriented family."

GENERAL

Co-ed K-8 Catholic parochial school (98% of students are Catholic). Founded in 1964. **Accreditation:** WASC (through 2002). **Nonprofit. Enrollment:** 315. **Average class size:** 30 in K, 36 in grades 1-8. **Length of school year:** 180 days. **Length of school day:** 8 a.m.-2:45 p.m. **Location:** In the Berryessa area of San Jose (off Highway 680).

STUDENT BODY

Geographic: Most students come from San Jose, Milpitas, and Fremont. **Ethnicity:** Approximately 47% Filipino, 22.5% Caucasian (non-Latino), 20% Asian or Pacific Islander, 7% Latino, 7% other, .09% African-American, .03% Native American, .01% Middle Eastern or East Indian. **Foreign students:** None. **Two f/t working parent families:** 78%. **Single parent families:** 22%.

ADMISSION

<u>Kindergarten</u>. **Application deadline:** Mid-February (check with school for exact date). **Age requirement:** 5 years old by September 1. **Application fee:** $35. **Application process:** Testing for readiness for academic program at St. Victor. Interview if necessary. **Preschools visited by admission director:** N/P. **Number of applications received:** 140 applications received last year for 40 spaces. **Preferences:** Siblings, parish members, children of alumni. <u>Other grades</u>. Application deadline, fee and evaluation/screening process are same as for K. **Admission test:** Teacher-developed admission test. **Test score/GPA cut-off:** N/P. **Estimated number of openings in grades other than K each year:** 1 or 2 "if lucky."

COSTS

Latest tuition: For in-parish Catholics, $2,890; for out-of-parish Catholics, $3,100; for others, $4,070. **Tuition payment plan:** Available. **Latest tuition increase:** N/P. **Sibling discount:** Substantial. **Percentage of students receiving financial aid:** .05%. **Average grant award:** N/P. **Number of full tuition grants:**

None. **Number of partial tuition grants:** 17, all for less than half-tuition. **Other information regarding financial assistance:** "Diocesan Scholarship Program for Catholic students."

PROGRAM AND PHILOSOPHY

<u>School's mission statement/goals.</u> "St. Victor Catholic School is committed to teaching the Christian message, building a faith community, offering service for others and providing academic excellence." [Statement of philosophy:] "St. Victor's School is dedicated to teaching the Catholic religion and promoting academic excellence. The school is an integral part of the whole parish family, providing an environment for the living out of Gospel values within the context of the multi-cultural Christian community." **Academic program. Approach to teaching reading:** "Use of basal reader and leveled reading. Reading promotes writing, and critical thinking." **Approach to teaching math:** "Combination of mastery of skills and problem solving." **Approach to technology and computer training:** "Full computer lab with 36 computers, at least one in each classroom. All are on-line. Keyboarding is taught routinely. Teachers use technology to enhance the academic program." **Other courses/offerings:** Art, music (two choirs), music in classroom, physical education and after-school athletics. **Special programs:** Seventh grade has a 4-day Christian living experience. After-school Homework Club for supervised study and Math Lab for one-on-one work in math. **Average nightly homework:** 10 to 15 minutes for K, 20 minutes for grade 1, 45 minutes for grades 2-3, 1 to 2 hours for grades 6-8. **Grading system for lower school:** O ("Outstanding"), S ("Satisfactory"), and N ("Needs Improvement"). **Grading system for middle school:** Letter grades (A-F). **Frequency of parent/teacher conferences:** "Once a year for all; others scheduled as needed or requested. Mid-term progress reports for all students and quarterly report cards." **Standardized test scores:** Provided to parents (child's scores). **High schools attended by recent graduates:** Bellarmine, Notre Dame, Presentation, Mitty, St. Francis and St. Lawrence. **Other indicators that the school is accomplishing its goals:** "High test scores, high retention and application rate; 80% of graduates are accepted into Catholic high schools."

ATHLETICS

Physical education program: Two instructors, no facility. Goal is "to teach skills for good physical maintenance, skills for play, sense of team work." **Interscholastic athletics:** Grades 5-8 compete in a league with other Catholic schools. Boys' teams compete in football, basketball and spring volleyball. Girls' teams compete in volleyball and basketball.

FACULTY

Gender: More than 99% female. **Ethnicity:** 74% Caucasian (non-Latino), 13% Latino, 13% Filipino. **Highest educational degree earned:** 62% Bachelor's, 38% Master's. **Credentials:** 12 teachers have California teaching credentials. Three have other credentials/training. **Teacher/student ratio:** Approx. 1:17. **Faculty selection and professional development:** "The Diocesan personnel office screens, interviews, [and makes] recommendations. Movement on salary scale is commensurate with education. In-service programs at school and off-site sponsored by Diocesan Department of Education and outside agencies are strongly encouraged for faculty."

EXTENDED CARE/AFTER-SCHOOL PROGRAMS

Extended care available from 7 a.m. until 6 p.m. for grades K-8. **Cost:** $4/hour or $100/week. **Drop-in:** Available. **No coverage on:** Holidays. **Snacks:** Provided. **Homework:** Homework Club for homework assistance. **Staff/child ratio:** 1:10. **After-school classes:** None.

CAMPUS LIFE

Facilities: The campus consists of three buildings: one for grades 5-8, offices and a resource classroom, a second building for grades 1-4 classrooms, and a third building for Kindergarten, the computer lab, library, and conference room. The school also has access to the Parish Hall, church and a large play area. **Meals:** One hot lunch per week. **Transportation:** No school-sponsored transportation. **Uniforms:** Required. **Co-curricular activities/clubs:** Includes student council. **Student support services:** "Must be obtained off-site." **Services for children with learning differences:** "Must be obtained off-site." **Counselor/student ratio:** N/A. **Policies regarding discipline, alcohol/drug use and abuse prevention and AIDS awareness:** "Part of curriculum in science, P.E./health and religion." **Summer programs:** None.

PARENT PARTICIPATION

40 hours/year required through services that directly benefit the students: library, hot lunch, sports, health room, and work parties. **Parent education:** Parent classes and retreats. **Fundraising:** Minimum annual contribution of $300/family.

WHAT SETS SCHOOL APART FROM OTHERS?

"We have a very strong academic program that is enriched by music, art and technology all set in a framework of nurturing values, respect and involvement."

HOW DO PARENTS/STUDENTS CHARACTERIZE THE SCHOOL?

"A safe place where individuals matter, teachers care and the Catholic faith and Christian values are taught."

SOUTH PENINSULA HEBREW DAY SCHOOL

1030 Astoria Drive
Sunnyvale, CA 94087
(408) 738-3060 *fax 408 738-0237*

Rabbi Charles Amberchick, *Head of School*

GENERAL

Co-ed PreK-8th grade Jewish day school (100% of students are Jewish). **Nonprofit. Accreditation:** Provisional CAIS. **Enrollment:** 310. **Average class size:** 15. **Length of school year:** Approximately 176 days. **Length of school day:** 8:30 am.-3:30 p.m. **Location:** In Sunnyvale, approximately 10 miles north of San Jose. Astoria is south of West Fremont Avenue, which is accessible from Highway 85.

STUDENT BODY

Geographic: Most students come from Sunnyvale and the neighboring cities of Palo Alto, San Jose, Cupertino, and Los Altos. **Ethnicity:** N/P. **Foreign students (I-20 status):** None. **Two f/t working/single parent families:** N/P.

ADMISSION

<u>Kindergarten.</u> **Application deadline:** March 1. **Age requirement:** 5 years old. **Application fee:** $50. **Application process:** "Includes interview." **Preschools visited by admission director:** None. **Number of applications received:** N/P. **Preferences:** Siblings. <u>Other grades.</u> **Application deadline:** March 1. **Application fee:** $50. **Application process:** School records, past test scores, interview, and visit. **Admission test:** None. **Test score/GPA cut-off:** None. **Estimated number of openings in grades other than K each year:** "Varies; limited in grades 1-4." **"We are looking for ..."** N/P. **"Our school best serves ..."** N/P.

COSTS

Latest tuition: $7,500 for K, $8,300 for G1-8. **Last tuition increase:** N/P. **Tuition payment plan:** Available. **Sibling discount:** For siblings, tuition is $6,850 for K, $7,450 for G1-8. **Financial aid:** N/P.

PROGRAM AND PHILOSOPHY

School's mission statement/goals. N/P. **Academic program.** N/P.

FACULTY

N/P.

CAMPUS LIFE
N/P.

WHAT SETS SCHOOL APART FROM OTHERS?
N/P.

HOW DO PARENTS/STUDENTS CHARACTERIZE THE SCHOOL?
N/P.

TRINITY SCHOOL

2650 Sand Hill Road
Menlo Park, CA 94025
(650) 854-0288 *fax (650) 854-1374*
www.trinity-mp.org

Mary Menacho, *Head of School*
Bonnie Slade-Castro, *Admissions Director* (bslade@trinity-mp.org)

We are looking for "students with an intellectual curiosity, a desire to learn, a willingness to participate. We seek to develop each child's skills in conjunction with well-defined academic standards."

GENERAL
Co-ed PreK-5th grade independent Episcopal school (25% of students are Episcopalian). The school has a junior K program. Founded 1961. **Nonprofit**, member CAIS. **Accreditation:** WASC, NAEYC (preschool). **Enrollment:** Approx. 200. **Average class size:** 18. **Length of school year:** 175 days. **Length of school**

day: 9 a.m.-12 p.m. (preschool), 8:15 a.m.-3 p.m. (elementary). **Location:** St. Bede's Church, Menlo Park, on Sand Hill Road, close to Interstate 280.

STUDENT BODY

Ethnicity: "15% students of color." **Geographic:** N/P. **Foreign students (I-20 status):** None. **Two f/t working/single parent families:** N/P.

ADMISSION

<u>Kindergarten.</u> **Application deadline:** Early February (check for date). **Age requirement:** N/P. **Application fee:** $50. **Application process:** Kindergarten applicants have one-on-one evaluation. **Preschools visited by admissions director:** None. **Number of applications received:** 50 applications received for 19 spaces last year; 12 spaces filled by students from the preschool program. **Preferences:** Siblings, children of faculty, Trinity preschool attendees. <u>Other grades.</u> **Application deadline:** Early February (check for date). **Application fee:** $50. Every applicant is screened on a Saturday morning in March. **Testing:** N/A. **Test score/GPA cut-off:** N/A. **Approximate number of openings each year:** Five. **"Our school best serves ..."** N/P.

COSTS

Latest tuition: $9,140 (full-day elementary). **Last tuition increase:** N/P. **Tuition payment plan:** Available. **Sibling discount:** None. **Percentage of students receiving financial aid:** 12%. **Average grant award:** $4,600. **Number of full tuition grants:** None. **Number of grants which are half tuition or more:** 24 (78%). **Other information regarding financial assistance:** All financial assistance is need-based.

PROGRAM AND PHILOSOPHY

<u>School's mission statement/goals.</u> "Trinity School encourages love of learning for children in preschool through grade five. The Trinity community upholds the values and traditions of the Episcopal Church and honors the role of the family in educating children. Trinity provides a comprehensive education program so that students can achieve their potential while preparing for future education challenges. We offer a nurturing, child-centered environment in which each student is challenged and encouraged to develop his or her potential. Our rich academic program emphasizes the development of strong scholastic skills, as well as curiosity, intellect, and reasoning." <u>Academic program.</u> **Approach to teaching reading:** Combination of phonics and literature. **Approach to teaching math:** Saxon Math. **Approach to technology and computer training:** The school has a computer specialist on the faculty and a technology committee. Computer lab and computers in the classroom. The Alpha-Smart (small, portable keyboard with memory for word processing) is used to teach keyboarding beginning in grade 3. All classes have access to the Internet and are networked. Computers are available for use at lunch and after school. **Other courses/offerings:** Spanish

(K-5), art (JK-5), athletics (JK-5), and library skills (JK-5). **Special programs:** Trinity school has a drama specialist for grades JK-5, field trips JK-5, overnight field trips in 4th and 5th grades, class projects days, Trinity Arts Night, community outreach, Halloween Carnival, book fair and family barbecues. **Average nightly homework:** Approximately 1 hour (individual work may vary). **Grading system:** Letter grades (grades 4 and 5 only). **Frequency of parent/teacher conferences:** One formal conference per year; "frequent" informal conferences and telephone availability. **Standardized test scores:** Reviewed at parent conference; school's overall performance reviewed at Parent Education Night. **Middle schools attended by recent graduates:** Castilleja, Crystal Springs, Menlo, St. Nicholas and Woodside Priory. **Other indicators that school is accomplishing its goals:** N/P.

ATHLETICS

Physical education program: The curriculum was developed by a full-time P.E. instructor to develop athletic and social skills, as well as flexibility, agility, motor development and overall body strength. **Interscholastic athletics:** None.

FACULTY

Gender: 83% female, 17% male. **Ethnicity:** "Faculty includes Asian/Pacific Islander, African-American, Caucasian, Latino and Native American ethnicities." **Highest degree held:** All have Bachelor's degrees, 28% hold Master's. **Credentials:** All elementary teachers hold California teaching credentials. **Student/teacher ratio:** 9:1. **Faculty training and professional development:** The school prefers to recruit faculty applicants who have teaching certificates; the school retains faculty with a "healthy professional development program."

EXTENDED CARE/AFTER-SCHOOL PROGRAMS

An extended care program is offered for all grades, JK-5, from 7:30 to 8:15 a.m. and after school from 3 p.m. to 6 p.m. **Cost:** N/P. **Drop in:** Available. **No coverage on:** School holidays. **Snacks:** Provided. **Homework:** Homework is encouraged and assistance is provided. **Staff/child ratio:** 1:10. **After-school classes:** Science, music (instrumental and vocal), sports and other subjects are offered at an additional cost.

CAMPUS LIFE

Facilities: The campus consists of a cluster of buildings around a courtyard, next to Trinity Church. It has a separate science/art room and multi-use building. The school's library has approximately 12,000 volumes and an automated catalog system. **Meals:** Hot lunch twice a week. **Transportation:** No school-sponsored transportation. **Uniforms:** Required. **Co-curricular activities/clubs:** Student council, student newspaper, Brownies. **Student support services:** N/P. **Services for children with learning differences:** Diagnosis only. **Policies regarding discipline, drug/alcohol use and abuse prevention and AIDS awareness:** N/P.

PARENT PARTICIPATION

Volunteers are encouraged to be part of the school program, and may work in the school library and classrooms, and at numerous school events and fundraisers. **Parent education:** Three sessions per year. **Fundraising:** Events include an annual fund drive, auction, and the Great Academic Brain Wave.

WHAT SETS SCHOOL APART FROM OTHERS?

"Trinity School provides a comprehensive academic program in a warm, supportive community for children in preschool through fifth grade. Small classes enable our teachers to provide a generous amount of individual attention, while an extraordinary level of parent involvement creates a strong sense of community."

HOW DO PARENTS/STUDENTS CHARACTERIZE THE SCHOOL?

"Trinity School is a stimulating place for children and parents alike. We are honored to say that our son is part of such a wonderfully nurturing, academic environment. In his time at Trinity he has blossomed. He's challenged by school and loves being there. It is exciting to watch him grow and learn."

WALDORF SCHOOL OF THE PENINSULA

11311 Mora Drive
Los Altos, CA 94024
(650) 948-8433 *fax (650) 949-2494*
linus@differnet.com/Waldorf School
waldorfschool@netscape.net

Mary Roscoe, *Administrator*
Debora Crosby, *Admissions Director*

We are looking for "children in the normal to gifted range of learning. We especially look for parents' support of the Waldorf philosophy and teaching methods." **Our school best serves** "all children whose parents are interested in an education which nurtures the whole human being: spiritual, emotional and physical."

GENERAL

Co-ed K-8 day school. Nonsectarian. Founded 1984. **Nonprofit. Accreditation:** Association of Waldorf Schools of North America (AWSNA) Sponsored School. **Enrollment:** 250. **Average class size:** 15-20 (K), 25 (grades K-5). **Length of school year:** 167 days. **Length of school day:** Grades K and 1, 8:30 a.m.-

12:30 p.m.; grades 2-8, 8:30 a.m.-2:45 p.m., Thursdays, 8:30 a.m.-12:30 p.m.
Location: In Los Altos, a residential community south of Palo Alto, near Interstate 280.

STUDENT BODY

Geographic: Students come from a wide area—Hillsborough to the north, San Jose to the south, Half Moon Bay to the east, Fremont to the west. **Ethnicity:** N/P. **Foreign students:** N/P. **Two f/t working/single parent families:** N/P.

ADMISSION

Kindergarten. Application deadline: December 15. **Age requirement:** K age range is 4 years, 9 months to 6 years. Child must be 4 years old before June 1st to be age eligible for 1st grade the following September. **Application fee:** $100, non-refundable. **Application process:** Child and parent interview with the class teacher. Child may be invited to visit the class following the interview. **Preschools visited by admission director:** "The Admissions Director will visit preschools for parent evenings to discuss Waldorf education." **Number of applications received:** 30 applications received for 50 spaces last year. 25 K spaces were filled by younger kindergarten class. **Preferences:** Siblings, transferring Waldorf students and children whose siblings have already graduated. **Other grades. Application deadline:** Applications to other grades can be submitted at any time, however the teachers determine how large their classes will be. Students are placed on the waiting list until a space becomes available. **Application fee:** $100, nonrefundable. **Application process:** The child and parents interview with the class teacher. Copies of student records, including any special testing, must be provided. Applicants are then invited to spend up to five days visiting the class. **Admission test:** None. **Test score/GPA cut-off:** None. **Estimated number of openings in grades other than K each year:** Two per class.

COSTS

Latest tuition: $7,265 (K-1), $8,050 (G2-8). **Last tuition increase:** Approximately 4.5%. **Tuition payment plan:** Available. **Sibling discount:** 10% for 1st sibling, 20% for 2nd sibling, and 30% for 3rd sibling. **Percentage of students receiving financial aid:** N/P. **Average grant award:** N/P. **Number of full tuition grants**: N/P. **Number of partial tuition grants:** N/P. **Other information regarding financial assistance:** The school has developed a tuition adjustment policy. Tuition adjustment applications are accepted after the class teacher has accepted the child. The policy works as follows: "If a family is unable to meet our tuition guidelines, the family completes a tuition adjustment application and meets with two members of our tuition adjustment committee. During this meeting both the school's budget and the family's budget are reviewed closely. The tuition is based on an understanding of the school as a whole. Neither the family nor the school determines the tuition, and neither maintains a comfortable position in this process; each stretches to meet the needs of the other. The final step in this meeting is to arrive, by consensus, at a tuition amount."

PROGRAM AND PHILOSOPHY

School's mission statement/goals. Waldorf Schools are based on the program created by Rudolf Steiner. "The Waldorf School of the Peninsula is dedicated to providing an education that affirms, embraces, and empowers the whole human being. With a reverence and love that acknowledges each child's uniqueness, we strive to awaken this individual potential as a means of helping develop complete human beings who are able to meet the future needs of humankind. To do this we are committed to our self-development and inner work based on the principles that guide Waldorf education. We encourage each individual in the community to understand and feel the meaning and value of the community as a living whole." The school's philosophy is reflected in a curriculum that "expands with the maturing child, matching themes that mirror the child's inner development with skills knowledge, and modes of expression appropriate to each age. Children record their lessons in special books that they create and illustrate themselves. In addition, the assumption of moral responsibility for one's action, a sense of stewardship for the earth, and caring relationships with others are emphasized and fostered." **Academic program. Approach to teaching reading:** N/P. **Approach to teaching math:** N/P. **Approach to technology and computer training:** "Because physical health and the developing senses are nourished by the child's imaginative and physical activity, we actively discourage young children from watching television, videos or playing computer games. The school asks for parents' support in this. No electronic media are used in the classroom." **Other courses/offerings:** Arts are integrated into the academic curriculum. Music, rhythm and movement are also emphasized. Offerings include recorder and flute (grades 1-8), Spanish (grades 1-8), handwork (grades 1-8), noncompetitive physical education (grades 1-8), gardening (grades 1-8), violin (grades 4-5), music ensemble (grades 6-8, elective), and athletic games coordinated with curriculum (grades 5-8). Three school assemblies each year to share artistic work with families. Grades 4-8 each perform end-of-the-year plays for the parents. Third grade spends a week at a farm. Fourth grade takes a trip to the gold country. Eighth grade has a graduation trip. **Average nightly homework:** None in grades 1-4; varied amounts in grades 5-8. **Grading system:** Written report on child's progress at the end of the year; parent conferences mid-year. **Grading system for middle school:** 7th and 8th grade transcript reports are graded based on the percentage of work completed and correct. A written evaluation supplements the grades. **Frequency of parent/teacher conferences:** One extensive conference mid-year plus five evening parent/teacher meetings. Others upon request. **Standardized test scores:** No standardized tests administered. **High schools attended by recent graduates:** SF Waldorf High School, Los Altos High School (public), Sierra High School (public), Leland High School (public), Gunn High School (public), Sacred Heart. **Other indications that the school is accomplishing its goals:** "High level of college acceptance and attendance by our alumni."

ATHLETICS

Physical education program: The school provides "games classes." Grades 1-4 play non-competitive games; grades 5-8 engage in competitions based on the curriculum with an emphasis on track and field rather than team sports. Eurhythmy, an art of movement to music and the spoken word, is practiced in grades 1-4. **Interscholastic athletics:** None.

FACULTY

Gender/ethnicity: N/P. **Highest educational degree earned:** N/P. **Credentials:** Teachers all have Bachelor's degrees plus Waldorf Teacher Training Certificates. **Teacher/student ratio:** N/P. **Faculty selection and development:** N/P.

EXTENDED CARE/AFTER SCHOOL PROGRAM

The after-school care begins at 12:30 p.m. and ends at 5:45 p.m., Monday-Friday. The after-school program is "a child-directed play experience." **Cost:** $4.25 per hour. **Snacks:** Provided. **Drop-in:** Available with 24-hour notice except emergencies. **No coverage on:** Thanksgiving, Christmas, New Year's Day and the 1st and last week of summer. **Homework:** Homework is encouraged for grades 5-8. **Staff/child ratio:** 1:10. **After-school classes:** N/P.

CAMPUS LIFE

Facilities: The campus has a "biodynamic garden" and walking access to a nature preserve. No library. **Meals:** None. **Transportation:** Carpools. **Uniforms:** Dress code. **Co-curricular activities/clubs:** None. **Student support services:** None. **Services for children with learning disabilities:** None. **Counselor/student ratio:** None. **Policies regarding discipline, drug/alcohol use or abuse and AIDS awareness:** "Age appropriate discipline. ... [The] science curriculum covers drug and alcohol use, abuse and sex education. We have had no problems with drug or alcohol abuse or usage. ... Warning, suspension or expulsion would be a consequence if needed." **Summer programs:** Yes, with aftercare program for GK-3.

PARENT PARTICIPATION

None required though parents support fundraising and serve on school committees. **Parent education:** Five required class meetings each year. **Fundraising:** Annual Holiday Faire created and run by parents. Scrip program. Parents are asked to participate in an Annual Giving campaign and are encouraged to support the fundraising program through the purchase of scrip certificates at cash value.

WHAT SETS SCHOOL APART FROM OTHERS?

"Waldorf education is the fastest growing independent movement worldwide. Teachers come to know the students extremely well and take long-term responsibility for their overall development. The class teacher is assigned in grade one and usually stays with the class through grade 8 with special subject teachers complementing the main course curriculum. The arts are an integrated part of all aspects of the academic curriculum. Music, drawing and painting are strong components of the curriculum and class experience. Creative thinking and creativity are nurtured through the arts."

How Do Parents/Students Characterize the School?

Parent response(s): "We appreciated the more humane speed of Waldorf education." "The school appeared stable and the staff supportive and friendly. We liked having one teacher to grow with our child throughout the years." "It was really Waldorf alumni that convinced me—I know several graduates, and they are all unusually self-directed and successful."

WOODLAND SCHOOL

360 La Cuesta Drive
Portola Valley, CA 94028
(650) 854-9065 *fax (650) 854-6006*
www.woodland-school.org

Lynne Nelson, *Director*
Lynn Presley, *Principal*
Janice Barkman, *Secretary and Admissions Director* (JBarkman@woodland-school.org)

General

Co-ed PreK-8th day school. Nonsectarian. Founded 1981. **Nonprofit. Accreditation:** N/P. **Enrollment**: 250. **Average class size:** 14-16. **Length of school year:** 183 days. **Length of school day:** 8:30 a.m.-3 p.m. **Location:** The school is located in the Ladera area of Portola Valley, just west of Interstate 280, Alpine Road exit.

Student Body

Geographic: Most students come from Menlo Park, Los Altos, San Carlos, Redwood City, Half Moon Bay, Fremont and Santa Clara. **Ethnicity:** "We are very diverse but do not classify students ethnically." **Foreign students (I-20 status):** None. **Two f/t working parent families:** 80%. **Single parent families:** 20%.

Admission

Kindergarten. **Application deadline:** None. **Age requirement:** None. **Application fee:** $35. **Application process:** 2-day student visit. **Preschools visited by** admission director: N/P. **Number of applications received:** Last year, 40 applications were received for 6 spaces. (Woodland School operates a PreK program.) **Preferences:** Siblings, alumni children, children of faculty. <u>Other grades.</u> **Application deadline:** As space becomes available. **Application fee:** $35. **Application process:** 2-day student visit. **Admission test:** None. **Test score/GPA cut-off:** None. **Estimated number of openings in grades other than K each year:** "Varies." **"We are looking for ..."** N/P. **"Our school best serves ..."** N/P.

COSTS

Latest tuition: $9,100 (K-4), $9,450 (G5-8), plus $750 registration fee. **Last tuition increase:** N/P. **Tuition payment plan:** One payment, two half payments or ten monthly payments. **Sibling discount:** 10%. **Percentage of students receiving financial aid:** N/P. **Average grant award:** N/P. **Other:** "We have a very generous financial aid package."

PROGRAM AND PHILOSOPHY

<u>School's mission statement/goals.</u> "The purpose of Woodland School is to provide a superior standard of education and to foster academic achievement and an appreciation of learning in each student." <u>**Academic program and philosophy.**</u> "Education is a lifelong process of which schooling is a necessary part. It forms the habit of learning and provides the means for continuing this habit throughout a lifetime. Woodland School strives to provide an atmosphere conducive to the acquisition of knowledge that will lead each student to find the joy and pleasure in learning. Mastery of basic skills is fundamental to the continuing progress of each student. While offering the basic skills, the curriculum is enriched and challenging for the more gifted." **Approach to teaching reading:** "Very phonetic. Starts in K." **Approach to teaching math:** "Individual instruction." **Approach to technology and computer training:** The computer lab, with 22 computers and an instructor, is available for use after-school and at lunchtime. Internet access. **Other courses/offerings:** French (Pre-K through 8), art, music (choral and instrumental for no additional fee), athletics, computer, dance, etiquette, and gymnastics. **Special programs:** All-school musical in the spring, Yosemite Institute (grades 5-6), Catalina Yachting (grades 7-8), Coloma overnight (4th grade), assemblies in drama, science and storytelling and field trips to farms, Stanford, and Davies Hall. **Average nightly homework:** 1.5 to 3 hours in grades 5-8. **Grading system for lower school:** 1-4. **Grading system for middle school:** A-F. **Frequency of parent/student conferences:** One to 2 conferences a year, 4 report cards. Notes, forms, and phone calls are also used to keep parents informed. **Standardized test scores:** Provided to parents (child's own scores). **High schools attended by recent graduates:** "We have many students in all the private high schools in the area." **Other indicators that the school is accomplishing its goals:** "Feedback from parents and alumni. [Our students are] well prepared!"

ATHLETICS

Physical education program: Combination of playing games (baseball, soccer, basketball, volleyball, tennis and hockey) and physical fitness. Huge area, coach, and gymnastics for grades K-4. **Interscholastic athletics:** Students compete in basketball and volleyball in G3-8. The school competes in a league with private and public schools. Various other after-school sports with coach until 5 p.m.

FACULTY

Gender: N/P. **Ethnicity:** N/P. **Highest educational degrees held:** N/P. **Credentials:** All hold California teaching credentials, many hold other credentials or training. **Teacher/student ratio:** 1:16 in the lower school, 1:12 in the middle school. **Faculty selection and professional development:** N/P.

EXTENDED CARE/AFTER-SCHOOL PROGRAMS

Extended care for all grades from 7:30 a.m. and after school to 5:30 p.m. **Cost:** $2.50/hour. **Drop-in:** Available. **No coverage on:** Legal holidays. **Snacks:** None provided. **Homework:** Homework time is voluntary; teacher provides assistance. **Staff/child ratio:** 1:15. **After-school classes:** "Sometimes."

CAMPUS LIFE

Facilities: The school occupies a former public school building on 10 acres with views of the nearby hills and Stanford. The campus has 20 classrooms, a library and a sports field. **Meals:** Lunches are available three times a week. **Transportation:** None. **Uniforms:** Required. **Co-curricular activities/clubs:** French, drama, student council, art, computer and yearbook. **Student support services:** None. **Services for children with learning differences:** None. **Counselor/student ratio:** None. **Policies regarding drug/alcohol use and abuse prevention and AIDS awareness:** N/P. **Summer programs:** 5-week program with academic morning and camp activity afternoon. $450-$750.

PARENT PARTICIPATION

No minimum. Volunteers used "very little." **Parent education:** None. **Fundraising:** No minimum contribution required. Events include a gift-wrap sale, a candy sale and an auction.

WHAT SETS SCHOOL APART FROM OTHERS?

"The caring and dedicated staff. Academic expectations are very high but not stressful."

HOW DO PARENTS/STUDENTS CHARACTERIZE THE SCHOOL?

"Children are happy to be at school. A happy and positive environment."

WOODSIDE PRIORY SCHOOL

302 Portola Road
Portola Valley, CA 94028-7897
(650) 851-8221 *fax (650) 851-2839*
www.woodsidepriory.com

Tim Molak, *Head of School*
Al D. Zapelli, *Director of Admission and Financial Aid*
(azapelli@woodsidepriory.com)

We are looking for "an understanding of the family's intent in choosing the school and compatibility of the student's beliefs with the school's philosophy." **Our school best serves** "a motivated and interested student who possesses a joy of learning and who can see that learning takes many different forms."

GENERAL

Co-ed day middle and high school with boarding for boys in grades 9-12. **Independent Catholic** (approximately 60% of the students are Catholic; the school is run by the order of St. Benedict). Founded 1957. **Nonprofit**, member CAIS, NAIS, BAIHS. **Accreditation:** WASC. **Enrollment**: 250 (grades 6-12). **Average class size:** 15-18. **Length of school year:** 180 days. **Length of school day:** 8 a.m.-3 p.m. **Location:** In Portola Valley, a semi-rural residential community west of Stanford University, 32 miles south of San Francisco and 30 miles north of San Jose. The school provides a shuttle bus to and from the Menlo Park CalTrain Station to accommodate students' commutes between San Francisco and San Jose.

STUDENT BODY

Geographic: Middle school students come from Portola Valley, Menlo Park, Redwood City, San Carlos, Belmont, Hillsborough, Los Altos, Los Altos Hills, Palo Alto, East Palo Alto, Mountain View, Sunnyvale, Santa Clara, San Jose, Milpitas, Fremont, Hayward, Half Moon Bay, La Honda and Woodside. **Ethnicity:** N/P. **Foreign students (I-20 status):** N/P. **Boarding students:** None in grades 6-8. **Two f/t working/single parent families:** N/P.

ADMISSION

Application deadline: Last week of January. **Application fee:** $40. **Application process:** Standardized test results (ERB, ISEE or Stanford Achievement Test, for example) given by student's current school must be sent with official transcript, teacher/principal recommendation, 3-year transcript, and a writing sample. A shadow visit will be scheduled. **Number of applications received:** 141 applications were received last year for 32 spaces in 6th grade, 17 applications for 4 spaces in 7th grade. (The school adds approximately 20-25 students at the 9th grade level.) **Test score/GPA cut-off:** No preset scores/cut-offs. "Many factors influence admissions decisions." **Preferences:** Siblings, children of faculty.

Costs

Latest tuition: For day students, $16,735 (includes books, fees and hot lunch). For boarding students $31,550. **Latest tuition increase:** 9.5%. **Tuition payment plan:** Available through Academic Management Services. **Sibling discount:** None. **Percentage of students receiving financial aid:** 23%. **Average grant award:** $5,000. **Number of full tuition grants in middle school:** None. **Other information regarding financial assistance:** The school uses the SSS service. Besides considering the amount recommended by SSS, the school will also take into consideration factors particular to the Bay Area and specific family situations in making awards. The school is preparing to launch a capital campaign.

Program and Philosophy

<u>School's mission statement/goals.</u> "The Woodside Priory School is a Catholic, co-educational, college preparatory school conducted by Benedictine monks who are assisted by religious laymen and women. The educational program and the school's sense of community take their character from St. Benedict's Rule for Monasteries and from the tradition of Benedictine education spanning fifteen centuries. That tradition embodies a love of learning and an intellectual and spiritual quest which supports and promotes individual and societal freedom. It encourages students to be creative, generous, and to mature emotionally which leads to higher standards of personal and societal responsibility. We hope to communicate to our students a love of God and a vision of life, of the universe, of society and of themselves which is stable in its foundations, adaptive in its applications, forward looking in its goals and satisfying in its fulfillment. Students, faculty and staff—supported by parents, alumni and benefactors—are dedicated to this dynamic process of education which regards learning and personal growth as a life-long endeavor." **Academic program.** College preparatory program. Courses are organized in seven academic divisions—English, science and technology, foreign languages, social studies, theology, fine and performing arts, and physical education. The school takes an interdisciplinary approach. Course offerings include math skills (6, 7, pre-algebra, algebra or geometry), ancient civilizations, English (writing and literature), science and technology, comparative cultures and languages, theology (revelation, community, and prayer), physical education, creative arts and music appreciation, drama, computer science. The foreign language program includes a "language arts wheel" in 6th grade that exposes the students to Japanese, German, French and Spanish. In 7th grade, students choose from Spanish, French or Japanese. Latin is offered with sufficient interest. **Approach to teaching reading/math:** N/P (middle school). **Approach to technology and computer training:** Over 120 personal computers are on campus, some in the writing lab and others in science labs, a computer center and the

library. Internet access. Student-prepared web site. A significant financial gift to the school provides funding for faculty training in computers and technology. **Other courses/offerings:** Outdoor education including a 6th grade trip to Big Basin and a 7th grade trip to Sacramento. Community Service is required of all students. The Campus Minister schedules retreats for students and faculty of each grade once each year. Beginning with the 8th grade, students spend retreat time in the Marin Headlands. **Average nightly homework:** Between 2-3 hours. **Grading system:** Letter grades (A-F). Progress reports and/or grade reports are issued 8 times per academic year. Progress reports are provided midway through each quarter to parents and are discussed with students through their advisors; grade reports are sent out quarterly. **Frequency of parent/teacher conferences:** Once, in fall. Parents may request additional conferences. Reports for the remaining three quarters are mailed to parents. The Academic Advising program keeps students informed of their academic progress. **Standardized test scores:** The Stanford Achievement Test is administered in grades 6-8. Scores are provided to parents. **High schools attended by recent graduates:** N/P. (The school consists of grades 6-12.) **Other indicators that school is achieving its goals:** "College acceptances (school includes list in information packet), 6-year WASC accreditation, SAT scores above national averages."

ATHLETICS

Physical education program: Part of curriculum. The program uses the high school facilities (including gym, playing fields, locker rooms, and outdoor pool). Health education is a component of the P.E. program. **Interscholastic athletics:** Member of Menlo Park Recreation League and the Small School Independent League. Middle school boys may participate in flag football, baseball, basketball, and soccer. Girls compete in volleyball, basketball, soccer, and tennis.

FACULTY

Gender: N/P. **Ethnicity:** N/P. The school has approximately 42 faculty members (high school and middle school) who teach at all levels. Many faculty members teach in multiple subject areas and/or work in administrative capacities. **Highest educational degree earned:** "Most hold advanced degrees." **Credentials:** "Most hold a teaching credential." Approximately 10 faculty members live on campus. **Teacher/student ratio:** 1:10 (most classes have fewer than 18 students). **Faculty selection and professional development:** Faculty are recruited through a departmental search, often national. Support of professional development includes a program funded by targeted donations to the school.

EXTENDED CARE/AFTER-SCHOOL PROGRAMS

N/P.

Campus Life

Facilities: 60-acre campus in Portola Valley with clusters of mostly one-story buildings containing classrooms, library, science laboratories, administration, chapel, 300-seat theater and dorms. Sports facilities include a 10,000 square foot gym, 25-meter pool, three soccer fields, two baseball diamonds, four tennis courts, and two basketball courts. The library has over 18,000 print volumes, plus periodicals and microfiche subscriptions. **Meals:** Lunch is included in the tuition. **Transportation:** Van transportation from/to the Menlo Park CalTrain station. **Uniforms:** None; "conservative" dress code. **Co-curricular activities/clubs:** Associated Student Body, student newspaper, yearbook, speech and debate, choir, orchestra, bike club, cross training club and stock market club. School dances sometimes include other private middle schools in the area. **Student support services:** Counseling. **Services for children with learning disabilities:** Academic advising department and learning resource specialist; no "pull-out programs." **Services for children with learning differences:** N/P. **Counselor/student ratio:** N/P. **Policies regarding discipline, drug/alcohol use and abuse prevention and AIDS awareness:** The school's general policy sets high standard of behavior and expectation that student conduct will "reflect mutual respect among and consideration for faculty, staff, administrators and fellow students." Formal disciplinary procedures are fully outlined in the parent/student handbook. A health and wellness program includes AIDS education. **Summer programs:** The campus is used for Camp Unique Summer Camp (not operated by school).

Parent Participation

No minimum required. Parents are "active and involved." **Parent education:** The school has a parent networking group that typically meets once a month with a speaker or other feature. **Fundraising:** Main events include the Annual Fund program, annual auction and golf tournament.

What Sets School Apart From Others?

The school is "not apologetic about its spiritual and religious component. ... The boarding program provides an international quality and a 24-hour feel to campus life. ... Families feel that the monastic community contributes to a strong sense of family."

How Do Parents/Students Characterize the School?

"The sense of community is warm and welcoming. The teachers are wonderful and very accessible; students feel comfortable approaching the teachers and administration with any concerns or questions."—7th grade parent
"The environment is friendly and nurturing and encourages individuality. The opportunity to interact with high school students in a small school provides access to good role models."—Sixth grade parent

ADDITIONAL SCHOOLS

There are literally hundreds of schools in San Mateo and Santa Clara counties and more being started every year. Listed below are additional schools, some of which were invited to be included in the full listing section of the book but chose not to be (for various reasons, including large wait lists, or in the case of some religious schools, a focus on serving their own parishes). We welcome the schools listed below to contact Pince-Nez Press to request a full listing in future editions.

San Mateo County

ALL SOULS CATHOLIC ELEMENTARY SCHOOL

479 Miller Avenue
South San Francisco, CA 94080
(650) 583-3562
Co-ed K-8 Catholic parochial school. Accreditation: WASC/WCEA. **Enrollment:** Approx. 320. **Tuition:** Approx. $3,000. Uniforms.

ALMA HEIGHTS CHRISTIAN ACADEMY

Elementary:
1295 Seville Drive
Pacifica, CA 94044
(650) 359-0555

Middle/High School:
1030 Linda Mar Blvd.
Pacifica, CA 94044
(650) 355-1935 *fax (650) 355-3488*

www.almaheights.org
David Welling, *Principal*
Co-ed K-12 Christian school. Founded 1955. **Accreditation:** ACSI. **Enrollment:** Approx. 284. **Application:** The application can be downloaded from school's website.

ALPHA BEACON CHRISTIAN SCHOOL

750 Dartmouth Avenue
San Carlos, CA 94070
(650) 592-2888 *fax (650) 592-5847*
www.alphabeacon.org
abcinfo@alphabeacon.org
Lillian Mark, *Principal*
Coed PreK-12 Christian school. Founded 1969. **Nonprofit. Accreditation:** ACSI. **Enrollment:** Approx. 250. "Alpha Beacon Christian School has served

thousands of families on the Peninsula with a strong, traditional Biblical-based education. ... As a notable distinction, Alpha Beacon is one of thirteen high schools in Northern California accredited by ACSI, which has a membership of 4,000 schools representing more than 800,000 students all over the world. ..." **Standardized tests:** "Annual Stanford Achievement Test scores in both elementary and high school have typically averaged one to two years above the national average test scores." **Approach to teaching reading:** "Phonics." **Approach for teaching math:** "Accelerated curriculum of traditional math." **Approach to technology:** "The school is in the process of equipping classrooms with computer laptops."

CHARLES ARMSTRONG SCHOOL
1405 Solana Drive
Belmont, CA 94002
(650) 592-7570 *fax (650) 592-0780*
www.charlesarmstrong.org
Rosalie Whitlock, Ph.D., *Head of School*
Tuck Geerds, *Director of Admissions*
Coed G1-8 school for children with learning disabilities/dyslexia. Founded 1968. **Accreditation:** WASC candidate. **Enrollment:** 215. **Tuition:** Approx. $14,000.

GERMAN-AMERICAN SCHOOL OF SAN FRANCISCO
275 Elliot Drive
Menlo Park, CA 94027
(650) 324-8617
Coed K-10 German school. Enrollment: Approx. 260. All classes in German. **Tuition:** Approx. $6,500.

GOOD SHEPHERD SCHOOL
909 Oceana Blvd.
Pacifica, CA 94044
(650) 359-4544
Coed K-12 Christian school. Accreditation: WASC. **Enrollment:** Approx. 350. **Tuition:** Approx. $3,300.

HERITAGE CHRISTIAN ACADEMY
1305 Middlefield Road
Redwood City, CA 94063
(650) 366-3842 *fax (650) 366-0790*
www.pcconline.org/christia/htm
onesimus@ix.netcom.com
Linda Packer, *Principal*
Coed PreK-12 Christian school, sponsored by Peninsula Christian Center. **Accreditation:** ACSI. **Enrollment:** Approx. 150. **School day:** 8:30 a.m. to 3 p.m.

Philosophy: "[W]e believe that each child is unique and special, created by God, Who loves and cares for him/her. We desire to work alongside parents, whom we recognize as those primarily responsible to nurture and train their sons and daughters." **Academic program:** Heritage Christian Academy presents the academic subjects and enrichment activities from a Christian perspective. Dedicated Christian teachers in a warm and caring atmosphere encourage students to honor God in all areas of their lives, including their studies and social relationships." **Extended care:** 7 a.m. to 6. p.m. for daycare.

HIGHLANDS CHRISTIAN SCHOOL
1900 Monterey Avenue
San Bruno, CA 94066
(650) 873-4090
vernita@churchofthehighlands.org
Vernita Sheley, *Superintendent/Principal*
Mary Van Maanen, *Assistant Administrator*
Gayla Hale, *Assistant Administrator*
Coed infants-G8 Christian school. Founded 1966. **Accreditation:** ASCI/WASC. **Enrollment:** Approx. 1,000.

HOLY ANGELS SCHOOL
20 Reiner Street
Colma, CA 94014
(650) 755-0220
Coed K-8 Catholic parochial school. Accreditation: WASC/WCEA. **Enrollment:** Approx. 320. **Tuition:** For in-parish, $2,420; for out-of-parish or nonparticipating, $3,170.

IMMACULATE HEART OF MARY
1000 Alameda de Las Pulgas
Belmont, CA 94002
(650) 593-4265
Coed K-8 Catholic parochial. Accreditation: WASC/WCEA. **Enrollment:** Approx. 300. **Tuition:** For in-parish, $2,720; for out-of-parish or non-participating, $3,170.

THE JEWISH DAY SCHOOL OF THE NORTH PENINSULA
800 Foster City Blvd.
Foster City, CA 94404
(650) 345-8900 *fax (650) 345-9596*
Mervyn K. Danker, *Principal*
Co-ed K-6 Jewish day school. Nonprofit. Accreditation: Provisional member, CAIS. **Enrollment:** 220. **Tuition:** Approx. $6,500.

MATER DOLOROSA SCHOOL

1040 Miller Avenue
South San Francisco, CA 94080
(650) 588-8175
Co-ed K-8 Catholic parochial school. Accreditation: WASC/WCEA. **Enrollment:** Approx. 250. **Tuition:** For in-parish, $2,750; for out-of-parish or non-participating, $3,190.

NATIVITY ELEMENTARY

1250 Laurel Street
Menlo Park, CA 94025
(650) 325-7304
www.nativityparish.org/school
Coed K-8 Catholic parochial school, administered and staffed by the Sisters of the Presentation of the Blessed Virgin Mary. **Accreditation:** WASC/WCEA. **Enrollment:** Approx. 275. **Tuition:** For in-parish, $3,090; for out-of-parish or non-participating, $3,440; for non-Catholics, $4,140. **Mission:** "Our chief goal is to produce boys and girls committed to Christian values. The curriculum is geared to challenging and encouraging each student to strive to reach their highest possible achievement. Our task and our commitment is to educate the whole child while recognizing and respecting the uniqueness and dignity of each individual, to integrate learning and living, and to refine our curriculum continually so as to prepare our students for the challenges and demands of tomorrow." **High schools:** "Ninety-nine percent of our graduates get into the high school of their choice." **Extended care. Learning differences:** Learning specialist, part-time speech therapist. **Approach to technology:** "Full-time computer teacher." **Support services:** School Counselor. **Meals:** Hot lunches. **Other:** After-school instrumental music program for G1-8; after-school sports program for G4-8; Scouts. **Summer program:** 9-week program.

OUR LADY OF ANGELS

1328 Cabrillo Avenue
Burlingame, CA 94101
(650) 343-9100
Co-ed K-8 Catholic parochial school. Accreditation: WASC/WCEA. **Enrollment:** Approx. 310. **Tuition:** For in-parish, $3,000; for out-of-parish or non-participating, $3,743.

Our Lady of Mercy

Seven Elmwood Drive
Daly City, CA 94015
(650) 756-3395
olmcath.org/school/index.html
Coed K-8 Catholic parochial school. Accreditation: WASC/WCEA. **Enrollment:** Approx. 600. **Tuition:** For in-parish, $3,500. **Philosophy:** "Our Lady of Mercy Catholic School community of faith provides for the growth of the whole child based on Catholic/Christian values. It nourishes the spiritual, intellectual, social, psychological and physical growth of each child. Our students are helped to develop their unique abilities and are prepared to succeed in future educational endeavors and to live effectively in the Church, civic and cultural communities." **Standardized tests:** "Our students score well above the national average on standardized achievement tests." **High schools:** "The majority of our graduates continue their academic success in one of the Bay Area Catholic High Schools." **Learning differences:** "Our Lady of Mercy has a full-time credentialed Special Education Teacher on staff to test, remediate and/or refer students with learning differences. **Student support:** A full-time counselor is available to help both students and their families at difficult times. **Extended care:** "The extended care program, designated 'The Clubhouse,' has been designed to create an extended family atmosphere for the students in Kindergarten through Fifth Grade who need quality care."

Our Lady of Mount Carmel

301 Grant Avenue
Redwood City, CA 94062
(650) 366-6127
Coed K-8 Catholic parochial school. Accreditation: WASC/WCEA. **Enrollment:** Approx. 300. **Tuition:** For in-parish, $2,990; for out-of-parish or non-participating, $3,590.

Our Lady of Perpetual Help School

80 Wellington Avenue
Daly City, CA 94014
(650) 755-4438
Coed K-8 Catholic parochial school. Accreditation: WASC/WCEA. **Enrollment:** Approx. 320. **Tuition:** For in-parish, $2,500.

Peninsula School

920 Peninsula Way
Menlo Park, CA 94025
(650) 325-1584
Coed nursery-8th grade alternative school. Tuition: Approx. $6,500.

St. Dunston School

1150 Magnolia Street
Millbrae, CA 94030
(650) 697-8119

Coed K-8 Catholic parochial school. Accreditation: WASC/WCEA. **Enrollment:** Approx. 312. **Tuition:** For in-parish, $2,980; for out-of-parish or non-participating, $3,930; for non-Catholic, $4,430.

St. Matthew's Catholic School

910 S. El Camino Real
San Mateo, CA 94402
(650) 343-1373

Coed K-8 Catholic parochial school. Accreditation: WASC/WCEA. **Enrollment:** Approx. 526. **Tuition:** Approx. $2,700.

St. Pius Elementary

1100 Woodside Road
Redwood City, CA 94061
(650) 368-8327

Coed K-8 Catholic parochial school. Accreditation: WASC/WCEA. **Enrollment:** Approx. 310. **Tuition:** $2,550 for in-parish.

St. Raymond School

1211 Arbor Road
Menlo Park, CA 94025
(650) 322-2312
www.straymong.org

Coed K-8 Catholic parochial school. Accreditation: WASC/WCEA. **Enrollment:** Approx. 270. **Tuition:** For in-parish, $3,900; for out-of-parish or non-participating, $4,750. **Philosophy:** St. Raymond Parish School is a "Christ-centered Community united in the Catholic faith. We believe that parents have the primary responsibility for the formation of their children's Christian values. The teacher and staff have unique roles, as professional educators, to support, enhance and complement that responsibility. The religious curriculum teaches the values, heritage, and traditions of the Catholic Church and provides opportunities to participate in prayer and charitable works. Our curriculum offers students the opportunity to develop self-esteem, mutual respect, and an appreciation of diversity."

ST. ROBERT SCHOOL
345 Oak Avenue
San Bruno, CA 94066
(650) 583-5065
www.saintroberts.org

Coed K-8 Catholic parochial school. Accreditation: WASC/WCEA. **Enrollment:** Approx. 315. **Latest tuition:** For in-parish, $2,820; for out-of-parish or non-participating, $3,096; for non-Catholic, $3,792. **Academic program:** "The instructional program at St. Robert School has a solid Christian orientation and continues to aim for intellectual excellence in the spirit of Gospel values. These goals are realized through an effective partnership of parents and dedicated faculty and staff. **Approach to teaching reading:** "A variety of teaching methodologies is used to ensure that the students receive a strong background in phonics, spelling, vocabulary, comprehension, creative writing, literature, and basic English grammar." **Approach to teaching math:** The mathematics curriculum begins with a foundation in pre-math skills with hands-on activities such as sorting, comparing, estimating and counting. Throughout the grades, this foundation is reinforced with basic computational skills and problem solving for everyday situations and culminates with an introduction to algebra. **Approach to technology:** Students in grades K-8 are instructed in computer literacy and basic keyboard skills in our computer lab. They utilize software programs to broaden and accelerate their learning in academic and enrichment areas. Classroom computers further enhance the learning experience as teachers integrate technology into the regular curriculum. **Extended care:** Available on all school days before and after school from 7:05 a.m. to 5:45 p.m. with supervised homework, free play, and socialization. **Faculty:** "Fully credentialed."

ST. VERONICA
434 Alida Way
South San Francisco, CA 94080
(650) 589-3909

Coed K-8 Catholic parochial school. Accreditation: WASC/WCEA. **Enrollment:** Approx. 320. **Tuition:** For in-parish, $2,928; for out-of-parish or non-participating, $4,428.

STANBRIDGE ACADEMY
515 East Poplar Avenue
San Mateo, CA 94401
(650) 375-5860 *fax (650) 375-5861*
www.stanbridgeacademy.org
info@stanbridgeacademy.org

Co-ed K-12 day school. Nonprofit. Nonsectarian. Founded in 1982. **Accreditation:** WASC. **Enrollment:** Approx. 80. **Latest tuition:** $14,500-$15,500. **Application fee:** $200. **Other costs:** $700 equipment fee. **Mission:** "Stanbridge

Academy is a private, nonprofit school for students with specific learning disabilities, primary grades through high school. We provide an experientially-based educational environment which fosters creativity, challenge, safety, and individual growth for students and staff. We strive to prepare our students to succeed academically and socially to their full potential." **Other:** Annual ski trip. **"We best serve ..."** "Appropriate candidates for Stanbridge Academy are of at least average intellectual potential, have suspected or diagnosed learning disabilities, and have no primary emotional or behavioral problems."

SANTA CLARA COUNTY

CANTERBURY CHRISTIAN SCHOOL
101 North El Monte
Los Altos, CA 94022
(650) 949-0909
Co-ed K-6 Christian school. Enrollment: Approx. 106. **Nondenominational.** Class size: 15. **Tuition:** Approximately $3,700. **Extended care:** To 5:30 p.m.

CANYON HEIGHTS ACADEMY
310 Easy Street
Mountain View, CA 94043
(650) 691-9373
Co-ed independent Catholic school, currently enrolling K-2. Founded 2000. "Academic excellence and Catholic values." The school has acquired 100 acres in the Cupertino foothills for a future site. At least some classes may be single-sex after grade 3. **Tuition:** Approx. $7,000.

CHALLENGER SCHOOLS
(locations with elementary programs)
1185 Hollenbeck Avenue
Sunnyvale, CA 94086
(408) 245-7170

2845 Meridian Avenue
San Jose, CA 95124
(408) 723-0111

711 East Gish Road
San Jose, CA 95112
(408) 998-2860

3880 Middlefield Road
Palo Alto, CA 94306
(650) 213-8248
www.challengerschools.com
California regional office: (408) 377-2300 *fax (408) 377-2498*
Coed preschool through 8th grade school (not at all campuses). **Enrollment:** Varies by campus. **Tuition:** Approximately $7,500. **Mission statement:** "Our mission is to prepare children to become self-reliant, productive individuals; to teach them to think, speak, and write with clarity, precision, and independence; and to inspire them to embrace challenge and find joy and self-worth through achievement."

CHRISTIAN COMMUNITY ACADEMY
1523 McLaughlin Avenue
San Jose, CA 95122
(408) 279-0846 *fax (408) 279-0185*
Kenneth G. Van Meter, *Principal*
Coed K-12 Christian school, sponsored by the Christian Community Church. Founded 1978. **Accreditation:** ACSI. **Enrollment:** Approx. 250.

EMERSON SCHOOL
4251 El Camino Real
Palo Alto, CA 94306
(650) 424-1267 *fax (650) 856-2778*
jaye@headsup.org
Coed G1-8 Montessori school. Year-round, all-day Montessori-based program. **Enrollment:** 60. **Tuition:** Approximately $11,000. **Extended care:** To 6 p.m. **Class size:** Average 19.

FRENCH AMERICAN SCHOOL OF SILICON VALLEY
1522 Lewinston Drive
Sunnyvale, CA 94087
(408) 746-0460
Co-ed PreK-4 French school. Enrollment: Approx. 120. **Tuition:** Approx. $8,300.

GERMAN SCHOOL OF SILICON VALLEY
310 Easy Street
Mountain View, CA 94043
(650) 216-9200 *fax (650) 216-9222*
www.ds-sv.org, team@ds-sv.org

Co-ed K-8 German school. Founded in 2000. Recognized as a German Foreign School. Core curriculum follows German college preparatory and is taught entirely in German. English language and literacy program.

HILLBROOK SCHOOL

300 Marchmont Drive
Los Gatos, CA 95032
(408) 356-6116
www.hillbrook.org
Coed JK-8 day school. Enrollment: Approx. 310. **Nonprofit**, member CAIS. **Tuition:** Approx. $11,000. **Uniforms. Transportation:** Bus service to designated areas. **Extended care:** Drop-in available.

HOLY SPIRIT ELEMENTARY SCHOOL

1198 Redmond Avenue
San Jose, CA 95120
(408) 997-5115
Co-ed K-8 Catholic parochial school. Founded in 2000. **Enrollment:** 325.

INTERNATIONAL SCHOOL OF THE PENINSULA

3233 Cowper Street
Palo Alto, CA 94306
(650) 328-2338
www.istp.org
admissions@istp.org
Co-ed PreK-8 day school. French section offering bilingual program for grades PreK-8th. Chinese section (Mandarin) offering bilingual program for PreK-4. **Nonprofit**, member of CAIS. **Accreditation:** WASC and the French National Ministry of Education. **Enrollment:** Approx. 400. **Tuition:** Approx. $10,000.

MILPITAS CHRISTIAN SCHOOL

3435 Birchwood Lane
San Jose, CA 94132
(408) 945-6530
Coed K-8 Christian school. Accreditation: WASC. **Tuition:** Approx. $4,000.

PRIMARY PLUS SCHOOL

3500 Amber Drive
San Jose, CA 95117
(408) 248-2464
www.primaryplus.com
Co-ed K-8 day school. Enrollment: Approx. 400. **Tuition:** Approx. $6,000.

Resurrection School

1395 Hollenbeck Avenue
Sunnyvale, CA 94086
(408) 245-4571 *fax (408) 245-4576*
www.resparish.org
resurrschool@connectin.com
Virginia Mirrione, *Principal*

Co-ed PreK-8 Catholic parochial school. Founded in 1965. **Accreditation:** WASC/WCEA. **Extended care. Enrollment:** Approx. 300. **Tuition:** $3,480 for in-parish, $4,940 for out-of-parish, and $5,140 for others. **Sibling discount:** Substantial. **Extended care:** 6 a.m.-6 p.m. **Mission statement:** "Resurrection School seeks to develop the individual student's full potential spiritually, mentally, morally, and physically by providing a Catholic education emphasizing religion, academics, technology, critical thinking, love of learning, self-esteem, and care and concern for others, with full support from parents and Parish Community in a Christ-centered, caring environment."

Sacred Heart School

13718 Saratoga Avenue
Saratoga, CA 95070
(408) 867-9241
www.sacred-heart.pvt.k12.ca.us/
Jane Daigle, *Principal*

Co-ed Catholic parochial school with Montessori preschool and K-8 elementary. Founded in 1956. **Accreditation:** WASC/WCEA. **Enrollment:** Approx. 360. **Tuition:** $4,075 for in-parish Catholic, $5,000 otherwise. **Sibling discount:** Substantial for Catholics only. **Mission statement:** "The mission of Sacred Heart School is to offer students a Catholic education from which they can draw the inspiration to live as Jesus did, to respect themselves and one another, and to become citizens of the Church and the world community. Sacred Heart School accepts the responsibility to lead students to the skills, knowledge and behaviors which will equip them to be resourceful and to meet life's challenges with faith and courage."

St. Andrew's Episcopal School

13601 Saratoga Avenue
Saratoga. CA 95070-5055
(408) 867-3785
Harry V. McKay, Jr., *Headmaster*

Co-ed PreK-8 independent Episcopal school. Nonprofit, member CAIS. **Enrollment:** Approx. 455. **Tuition:** Approx. $3,000-$8,000.

St. Christopher School

2278 Booksin Avenue
San Jose, CA 95125
(408) 723-7223 *fax (408) 978-5458*
www.stchris.diosj.pvt.k12.ca.us/
Arlene Ernst, *Principal*

Co-ed K-8 Catholic parochial school. Founded in 1955. **Accreditation:** WASC/WCEA. **Enrollment:** Approx. 600. **Tuition:** For K. $2,220; for G1-8, $3,350 for in-parish, $4,000 otherwise. **Sibling discount:** Substantial. **Mission statement:** "The St. Christopher School philosophy is based on the belief that a Catholic education is developed in a parish school, supported by a faith community. Parents are the primary educators of their children. The development of Catholic citizens is the joint responsibility of the parents, the school, and the Church. The fulfillment of developing the whole child—the ideas, the attitudes, the habits, the values, the principles—can be achieved through quality Catholic education, which centers around the message of Jesus. Recognizing the potential of the students for leadership, they are encouraged to appreciate their own self-worth, continue to develop their talents, and become aware of their responsibilities to self, God, Church, society, and earth."

St. Clare's School

725 Washington Street
Santa Clara, CA 95050
(408) 246-6797 *fax (408) 246-6726*
Kathy Almazol, *Principal*

Co-ed K-8 Catholic parochial school. Founded in 1856, reestablished in 1925. **Accreditation:** WASC/WCEA. **Enrollment:** Approx. 300. **Tuition:** For Catholics, $3,390 for one child, $5,340 for two, and $7,290 for three or more. **Extended care:** 6:30 a.m.-8:10 a.m., 3 p.m.-6 p.m. **Mission statement:** "We at St. Clare's School believe that Catholic education is an expression of the mission entrusted by Jesus Christ to the Church He founded. We strive to prepare our students to proclaim the Gospel message of Jesus and to put this proclamation into action. ... As educational ministers, we seek to create a Christ-centered environment for all children who come to us. We provide an environment that is supportive and nurturing for all students and families. Throughout the curriculum, we foster the growth and development of the whole child, spiritually, academically, socially, psychologically, and physically. Our aim is to encourage all students to develop respect for self and others, leading to an appreciation of the uniqueness of all God's creation. Our mission is to create a community of faith and love."

St. Cyperian Elementary School

195 Leota Avenue
Sunnyvale, CA 94086
(408) 738-3444 *fax (408) 733-3730*
Kay Ingalls, *Principal*
Co-ed K-8 Catholic parochial school. Founded in 1968. **Accreditation:** WASC/
WCEA. **Enrollment:** Approx. 300. **Tuition:** For K, $2,426 for in-parish, $2,892
for out, and $3,328 for non-Catholic; for G1-8, $2,674 for in-parish, $3,141 for
out-of-parish, and $3,577 for non-Catholic. **Sibling discount:** Substantial for
Catholics only. **Mission statement:** "St Cyperian Catholic School is a dynamic
witness to the commitment and generosity of its faith community. It is our sol-
emn pledge of hope for the creation of a better future by forming our young
members according to Gospel values. Gospel values are integrated and insepa-
rable as we strive to avoid compartmentalizing life and learning. Our mission is
to assist parents in transmitting the message of Christ, in providing opportunities
to live in community, and in calling forth to respond in joyful service."

St. Elizabeth Seton

1095 Channing Avenue
Palo Alto, CA 94301
(650) 326-9004
Co-ed K-8 Catholic parochial school. Accreditation: WASC/WCEA. **Enrol-
ment:** Approx. 250. **Tuition:** $2,120 for 1 child, $3,390 for 2, $4,240 for 3+.

St. Francis Cabrini School

15325 Woodard Road
San Jose, CA 95124
(408) 377-6545 *fax (408) 377-8491*
www.sfcschool.org
SFCschool@aol.com
Mrs. Yvonne Gomez, *Principal*
Coed PreK-8 Catholic parochial school. Sponsored by the Dominican Sisters
of San Jose. Founded 1962. **Accreditation:** WASC/WCEA. **Enrollment:** Approx.
684. **Tuition:** For K, $2,550 for all; for G1-8, $3,200 for in-parish, $3,500 for
out-of-parish, and $3,680 for non-Catholics. **Sibling discount:** Substantial. **Ex-
tended care:** 6:30 a.m.-6 p.m. **Mission statement:** "St. Francis Cabrini is committed to developing the whole child by supporting the principles of the Catholic faith and by providing a solid academic education. Our goal is to provide both
the opportunity and the motivation for a child to develop spiritually, intellectually, physically, and socially." **Program:** "Daily religion and family life class, interactive science program, music, art and computer classes, whole language ori-
entation, enrichment and remedial classes, advanced junior high math classes,
extended day care, separate primary/middle school, student council, community

outreach, junior high humanities, yearbook, newspaper, liturgies, retreats, field trips, summer school, summer camp, Scouting, tutorials in 4-8 grade."

St. John the Baptist School

360 South Abel Street
Milpitas, CA 95035
(408) 262-8110 *fax (408) 262-0814*
www.sjbs.org
info@sjbs.org
Judith Perkowski, *Principal*
Co-ed Pre-K-8 Catholic parochial school. Founded in 1987. **Accreditation:** WASC/WCEA. **Enrollment:** Approx. 340. **Tuition:** For G1-8, $3,375 for in-parish, $3,675 for out-of-parish, and $3,975 for non-Catholics. **Sibling discount:** Substantial. **Extended care:** 6:30 a.m.-6 p.m. **Mission statement:** "Established in 1987, St. John the Baptist School serves the families of Milpitas and the Santa Clara Valley, with its central purpose being to assist parents in the Christian education of their children. Our community reflects the multi-cultural and multi-economic richness of the area where safe, nurturing surroundings provide students with the opportunities to reach their full potential. Aware of this partnership in the development of a whole child, our aim is to provide an educational environment that incudes all dimensions of human life—spiritual, moral, intellectual, and social. ..."

St. John Vianney School

4601 Hyland Avenue
San Jose, CA 95127
(408) 258-7677 *fax (408) 258-5997*
www.sjvsj.org
stjohnviansc@impresso.com
Sr. Michele Anne Murphy, *Principal*
Coed K-8 Catholic parochial school. Founded in 1954. Sponsored by the Sisters of the Presentation of the Blessed Virgin Mary. **Accreditation:** WASC/WCEA. **Enrollment:** Approx. 600. **Tuition:** For K, $2,360 for one in-parish child, $2,680 otherwise; for G1-8, $2,800 for one in-parish child, $3,580 for all others. **Sibling discount:** Substantial. **Extended care:** 7 a.m.-6 p.m. **Technology:** Ethernet network to all classrooms. **Mission statement:** "St. John Vianney Catholic School is committed to developing a community grounded on Gospel values in which a diverse group of students expands upon their gifts and recognizes their uniqueness in order to become self-directed, active learners in an interdependent world."

St. Joseph Elementary School

1120 Miramonte Avenue
Mountain View, CA 94040
(650) 967-1839 *fax (650) 691-1530*
www.sjmv.org
info@sjmv.org
Leonor Bolle, *Principal*
Coed K-8 Catholic parochial school. Founded in 1952. **Accreditation:** WASC/ WCEA. **Enrollment:** Approx. 300. **Location:** At the border of Mountain View and Los Altos, in a wooded residential area next to St. Francis High School, a large (1,455 students) Catholic high school. **Tuition:** For K, $2,360 for in-parish, $2,730 for out-of-parish, and $3,020 for non-Catholic; for G1-8, $3,130 for in-parish, $3,485 for out-of-parish, and $4,620 for non-Catholic. **Application fee:** $45. **Sibling discount:** Substantial. **Mission statement:** "We at St. Joseph School, in partnership with parents, pride ourselves in educating the whole child in an environment where spiritual growth, academic excellence and an appreciation of multi-cultural values are fostered. Our commitment in educating the whole child is based on the traditional Catholic values where the spiritual, social, emotional and physical growth is supported and nurtured."

St. Leo the Great School

1051 W. San Fernando Street
San Jose, CA 94126
(408) 293-4846 *fax (408) 293-5855*
www.stleos.pvt.k12.ca.us
Phyllis Taurosa, *Principal*
Co-ed K-8 Catholic parochial school. Founded in 1916. **Accreditation:** WASC/ WCEA. **Enrollment:** Approx. 275. **Tuition:** $3,018 for one child (in-parish Catholic), $3,520 otherwise. **Sibling discount:** Substantial. **Extended care:** 7 a.m.-6 p.m. **Mission statement:** "The mission of St. Leo the Great School is to create a Catholic environment and an academic atmosphere in which parents are recognized as the primary educators of their children. Both parents and staff foster in the students a love of learning, self-confidence, and a sense of responsibility to help the students discover and use their God-given potential."

St. Mary's School

30 Lyndon Avenue
Los Gatos, CA 95030
(408) 354-3944 *fax (408) 395-9151*
stmarylgsch@impresso.com
Sister Nicki Thomas, SNJM, *Principal*
Co-ed K-8 Catholic parochial school. Founded in 1952. Sponsored by the Sisters of the Holy Names of Jesus and Mary. **Accreditation:** WASC/WCEA.

Enrollment: Approx. 300. **Tuition:** For K, $2,940 for in-parish; for G1-8, $2,940 for in-parish, $3,610 for out-of-parish, and $4,430 for non-Catholic. **Sibling discount:** Substantial. **Extended care:** To 6 p.m., school days only. **Mission statement:** "St. Mary's Parish School is a Christian Community that teaches Catholicism as a way of life. In partnership with the parents, our school fosters an appreciation for learning and provides its students with an outstanding education. St. Mary's students develop a sense of responsibility to God, themselves, their families, and their community."

St. Nicholas School

12816 South El Monte Avenue
Los Altos, CA 94022
(650) 941-4056 *fax (650) 917-9872*
Mary Merkert, *Principal*
Co-ed K-8 Catholic parochial school. Founded in 1959. **Accreditation:** WASC/WCEA. **Enrollment:** Approx. 300. **Tuition:** For K, $2,850 for parish child, $4,300 otherwise; for G1-8, $3,650 for parish child, $5,200 otherwise. **Sibling discount:** Substantial. **Application fee:** $35. **Uniforms:** Required. **Mission statement:** "As a Catholic school, our mission is to assist our students in achieving their full potential spiritually, academically, emotionally, and physically. We provide a Christ-centered environment where we nurture the individual's learning style. The St. Nicholas School community actively participates in the Gospel mission to serve others by involvement in the current issues of social justice." Art, music and P.E. are in the curriculum at all grade levels. **Foreign languages:** "In curriculum for G7-8; elective for K-6." **Extended care:** Extended care is available as well as an after-school sports program for G4-8. **Campus:** "State-of-the-art Technology Center and newly built science facility. Extensive library."

St. Patrick School

51 North 9th Street
San Jose, CA 95112
(408) 283-5858 *fax (408) 283-5852*
John Bracco, *Principal*
Mrs. Ruth Lopez, *Admissions*
Co-ed Pre-K-8 Catholic parochial school. Founded in 1925. **Accreditation:** WASC/WCEA. **Enrollment:** Approx. 300. **Tuition:** For Pre-K and K, $2,380 for Catholic, $2,620 for non-Catholic; for G1-8, $2,662 for in-parish, $3,062 otherwise. **Sibling discount:** Substantial. **Extended care:** 7 a.m.-6 p.m.

St. Simon School

1840 Grant Road
Los Altos, CA 94024
(650) 968-9952 *fax (650) 988-9308*
www.stsimon.com
Sister Margaret Rose Adams, IHM, *Principal*
Co-ed K-8 Catholic parochial school. Founded in 1961. Sponsored by the Sisters, Servants of the Immaculate Heart of Mary, PA. **Accreditation:** WASC/WCEA. **Enrollment:** Approx. 585. **Tuition:** For K, $2,410; for G1-8, $3,120 for in-parish child, $3,590 for out-of-parish child, and $4,030 for a non-Catholic child. **Sibling discount:** Substantial. **Uniforms:** Required. **Extended care:** 7 a.m.-6 p.m. **Mission statement:** "St. Simon Catholic School, in partnership with each school family, strives to form a Community of Faith dedicated to living and teaching the message and mission that Jesus Christ entrusted to His Church. We, therefore, are committed to educating the whole child in a nurturing environment which reflects the Gospel message and fosters each student's spiritual, intellectual, emotional, social, aesthetic, and physical growth. In accordance with each child's gifts and abilities, we strive to provide the student with the skills needed to become a faith-filled, respectful, responsible individual and a productive member of his/her family, Church, community and society."

Sierra School

220 Blake Avenue, B
Santa Clara, CA 95051
(408) 247-4740
Co-ed K-12 day school. Accreditation: WASC candidate. **Tuition:** Approx. $7,000.

Silicon Valley Academy

1095 Dunford Way
Sunnyvale, CA 94087
408-243-9333
Co-ed K-7 Islamic school. Enrollment: Approximately 150. **Tuition:** K, $375/month; 1st-7th, $300/month for one child, $275/month each for 2 or more.

Southbay Christian School

1134 Miramonte Avenue
Mountain View, CA 94040
(650) 961-9485
Co-ed K-7th Christian school. Accreditation: WASC. **Enrollment:** Approx. 400. **Tuition:** $4,000-$8,000.

Valley Christian Schools

1570 Branham Lane
San Jose, CA 95118
(408) 978-9955
Co-ed K-12 Christian school. Accreditation: WASC.

Yavneh Day School

14855 Oka Road
Los Gatos, CA 95032
(408) 358-3413 *fax (408) 356-2324*
Elizabeth Michael, *Head of School*
Co-ed K-5 day school. Nonprofit, provisional member, CAIS. **Enrollment:**
128. **Tuition:** Approx. $7,600.

Appendix

Average Class Size

[Ed. Note: Average size is based on best available information from school; it does not take into account use of aides and specialists.]

<10	Los Altos Christian (small and special education classes)
11-15	Castilleja, Crystal Springs, Hilldale, Odyssey, SPHDS, Woodland
16-20	Girls' MS, Harker, Menlo, Nueva, Phillips Brooks (K-2), MPJDS (G6-8), Pinewood, Trinity, Waldorf (K), Woodside (15-18)
21-25	Los Altos Christian (large and general education classes), Phillips Brooks (grades 3-5), MPJDS (K-5), Redeemer, St. Joseph (Atherton), St. Matthew's Episcopal, Waldorf (G1-5)
26-30	Five Wounds, St. Victor (K)
31-35	Holy Family, Most Holy Trinity, Notre Dame, St. Justin, St. Joseph (Cupertino), St. Lawrence, St. Lucy, St. Martin of Tours, St. Martin
>35	Queen of Apostles, St. Catherine of Siena, St. Charles, St. Gregory, St. Victor (G1-6)
N/P	Carey, CIS, Keys

Foreign Languages Offered/Grades

[Ed. Note: Based on school responses and other sources; language programs in schools are subject to change due to student interest and teaching staff availability.]

Spanish
Carey (pre-K +), Castilleja, CIS, Crystal Springs, Girls' Middle School, Harker (1+), Hilldale, Keys, Menlo, Notre Dame (G1+), Nueva (K-5), Mid-Peninsula Jewish Community Day School (G8), Phillips Brooks, Redeemer Lutheran, St. Catherine of Siena, St. Justin, St. Lawrence (G6+), St. Martin of Tours (G7-8), Trinity, Woodland, Woodside Priory

French
Carey (Pre-K+), Castilleja, Crystal, Harker (G6+), LACS (after-school), Menlo, Phillips Brooks, Pinewood (G1-6), St. Martin of Tours (lower), St. Matthew's Episcopal (PreK+), Woodside Priory, French-American*, International School*

Japanese
Castilleja, CIS, Harker (G6+), Menlo, Nueva (G6+), Odyssey, St. Lawrence (G1-5), Woodside Priory

Latin
Castilleja, CIS (middle school), Crystal, Menlo, Woodside Priory (with sufficient student interest)

Portuguese
Five Wounds (after-school)

Italian
St. Catherine of Siena

Hebrew
Mid Peninsula Jewish Day School, South Peninsula Hebrew Day School,
Yavneh Day School

German
German-American School of San Francisco*

Chinese (Mandarin)
International School of the Peninsula*

* indicates bilingual or immersion program

SCHOOL SIZE (APPROX. ENROLLMENT)

[Note: Enrollment figures are based on most recent information provided
by school. In some cases, total may include pre-school and/or high
school enrollment.]

< 100	Children's International, Emerson, Stanbridge, Odyssey
101-200	Carey, Canterbury, French-American, Girls' Middle School, Heritage Christian, Hilldale, Keys, MPJCDS, Redeemer Lutheran, Silicon Valley Academy, Trinity, Yavneh Day School
201-300	Alpha Beacon, Alma Heights, Charles Armstrong, Christian Community Academy, Five Wounds, German-American School, Immaculate Heart of Mary, Jewish Day School of the Northern Peninsula, Los Altos Christian School, Mater Dolorosa, Menlo, Most Holy Trinity, Nativity, Notre Dame, Phillips Brooks, Pinewood, Resurrection, St. Clare, St. Cyperian, St. Elizabeth Seton, St. Joseph (Mountain View), St. Leo, St. Mary's, St. Matthew's Episcopal, St. Nicholas, St. Patrick, St. Raymond, SPHDS, Waldorf, Woodland, Woodside Priory
301-400	Castilleja, Crystal Springs, Good Shepherd, Hillbrook, Holy Angels, Holy Spirit, International School, Nueva, Our Lady of Mount Carmel, Our Lady of Perpetual Help,

Primary Plus, Queen of Apostles, Sacred Heart,
St. Catherine of Siena, St. Charles, St. Dunston,
St. Gregory, St. John the Baptist, St. Joseph of Cupertino,
St. Joseph's (Atherton), St. Justin, St. Lucy, St. Martin,
St. Pius, St. Robert, St. Veronica, St. Victor, South Bay
Christian, South Peninsula Hebrew Day School

401-500 St. Andrew's Episcopal, St. Lawrence Elementary and Middle School

501 and over Harker, Highlands Christian, Holy Family, Our Lady of Mercy, St. Francis Cabrini, St. Christopher, St. Matthew's Catholic, St. Simon, St. John Vianney

N/P Challenger Schools (multiple campuses), Milpitas Christian School, Peninsula School, Valley Christian, Sierra School

TEACHER/STUDENT RATIO

1:6	Girls' Middle School
1:8	Pinewood, Nueva
1:8.5	Menlo
1:9	Trinity, CIS, Crystal Springs, Harker (upper), Los Altos Christian ("small" classes), Phillips Brooks, Waldorf
1:10	Woodside Priory
1:11	Harker (lower), Carey, MPJCDS (lower), Odyssey
1:12	St. Martin of Tours, Hilldale, MPJCDS (upper), Notre Dame
1:15	St. Justin
1:16	Woodland (lower), Five Wounds (lower), St. Lawrence (lower)
1:17	St. Victor
1:17.5	St. Justin (G1-2)
1:18	St. Gregory
1:18.5	Queen of Apostles (lower)
1:24	Redeemer, Five Wounds (middle), Los Altos Christian ("large" classes)
1:25	Holy Family, Most Holy Trinity, Queen of Apostles (middle), St. Charles, St. Justin (3rd-8th), St. Lucy
1:35	St. Martin, St. Catherine, St. Gregory (middle), St. Joseph of Cupertino (middle)
1:36	St. Joseph of Cupertino (lower)

NOTES

NOTES

NOTES

NOTES

NOTES

NOTES

NOTES

NOTES

Other Books Published by Pince-Nez Press

Pince-Nez Press school guides are independent guides written by parents and educational consultants. They include discussions of how to choose the right school, profiles of schools, and important advice about the application process. They are based upon information provided by the schools, visits to most schools, and interviews with admission directors and heads of the schools.

USE THE ORDER FORM ON THE FOLLOWING PAGE
TO ORDER ANY OF THESE BOOKS BY CHECK
—OR ORDER WITH A CREDIT CARD ON OUR WEB SITE:
www.pince-nez.com

Private High Schools of the San Francisco Bay Area (Second Edition)
$21.95
By Susan Vogel   ISBN: 0-9648757-9-9
More than 50 private high schools in the Bay Area from Marin through San Jose and the East Bay. SATs and colleges enrolled in. Free updates and map.

High School Admission Workbook
$14.95
By Susan Vogel
Available only from Pince-Nez Press (not in bookstores). This 45-page wire bound workbook helps parents and kids prepare for and organize the grueling high school admission process.

Finding a Preschool for Your Child in San Francisco (Second Edition)
$19.95
By Lori Rifkin, Ph.D., Vera Obermeyer, Ph.D., and Irene Byrne
ISBN 0-9648757-2-1
More than 150 private and public preschools, how to choose a preschool, kindergarten readiness, and more. New, expanded second edition.

Private Schools of San Francisco and Marin Counties (K-8)(4th Edition)
$19.95
By Susan Vogel   ISBN 1-930074-02-6
More than 80 private elementary schools. This new, expanded 4th Edition adds schools in Marin County and doubles the amount of information on each school.

Finding a Nanny For Your Child in the San Francisco Bay Area
$16.95
By Alyce Desrosiers, LCSW   ISBN 1-930074-00-X
Practical advice and emotional support to help parents make the right choices. Includes essential local resources, such as where to post ads.

ORDER FORM

See descriptions of books on previous page

(or order with a credit card at www.pince-nez.com)

Private High Schools of the San Francisco Bay Area (2nd Ed.)
___ copy(ies) at $21.95 (8.5" x 5.5" bound book) $_____

High School Admission Workbook
___ copy(ies) at $14.95 (8.5" x 11" wire bound) $_____

Finding a Preschool for Your Child in San Francisco (2nd Ed.)
___ copy(ies) at $19.95 (8.5" x 5.5" bound book) $_____

Private Schools of San Francisco & Marin Counties (K-8)
___ copy(ies) at $19.95 (8.5" x 5.5" bound book) $_____

SUBTOTAL $_____

ADD sales tax (8.5% for San Francisco) $_____

ADD shipping/handling: for the first book,
$2.50 for book rate or $4.00 for priority rate $_____

for each additional book, add $.75 for book rate
or $1.00 for priority $_____

If you want the book(s) sent to an address other than the one on your check, please provide it:

Name:_____

Address: _____

City: _____

State: _____ Zip: _____

Mail this order form and your check made out to Pince-Nez Press to:

Pince-Nez Press/Order
1459 18th St.
PMB No. 175
San Francisco, CA 94107

Questions? Call (415) 267-5978